The book for every woman who has
ever asked herself . . .
WHY DO I THINK I AM NOTHING
WITHOUT A MAN?

by Dr. Penelope Russianoff

"READABLE AND USEFUL . . . Many women will identify with this book."

—Carly Simon

"A VERY PRACTICAL AND POSITIVE BOOK on the necessity of being your own person before you can have a good relationship. Loving, straightforward, and at times even humorous . . . I strongly recommend it."

—Claudia Weill

"I thoroughly enjoyed reading Penny Russianoff's new book . . . She offers practical advice to those who would like to lead rich, full lives, without or with spouse or lover."

—Arlene Alda

"Dr. Russianoff shows us how well she understands the world of women. This useful, informative book provides insights which will help the reader become emotionally strong and independent. Dr. Russianoff is a noted psychologist who knows firsthand whereof she writes."

—Florence L. Denmark, Ph.D., Past President
American Psychological Association

"I recommend this common sense addition to feminist literature about how to lead a fulfilled life without being over reliant on a man."

—Betsy Mazursky

"An important book for women but I recommend it to men, too."

—Paul Mazursky

Why Do I Think I Am Nothing Without a Man?

Penelope Russianoff, Ph.D.

BANTAM BOOKS
TORONTO · NEW YORK · LONDON · SYDNEY

None of the "patients" discussed in this book are based on any one individual. All names are fictitious and all case histories are of the author's creation based on the composite of her professional experience.

WHY DO I THINK I AM NOTHING WITHOUT A MAN?

Bantam Hardcover edition / May 1982

2nd printing . . . June 1982
3rd printing . . . June 1982
4th printing . . . September 1982
5th printing . . . December 1982

Bantam rack-size edition / May 1983

Library of Congress Cataloging in Publication Data
Russianoff, Penelope.
Why do I think I am nothing without a man?
1. Women—Psychology. 2. Women—Employment. I. Title.
HQ1206.R83   155.6'33   81-15033
ISBN 0-553-23271-1   AACR2

Published simultaneously in the United States and Canada

PRINTED IN THE UNITED STATES OF AMERICA

H   0 9 8 7 6 5 4 3 2

To my husband,
LEON RUSSIANOFF,
who puts up with my insecurities
and doubts, who discourages
desperate dependency, and who
lovingly supports my undependence,
curiosity, exploration, and
the risk-taking paths that my career
of clinical psychology has con-
tinuously set before me.

Acknowledgments

In the spring of 1979, my friend Kris Filner of the YWCA Women's Center asked me to give a short lecture series. "Why Do I Think I'm Nothing Without a Man?" was the first of these. The attendance and response resulted in the decision to put this material in book form.

Ruth Van Doren, Director of the Human Relations Center, and Alan Austill, Dean of the New School for Social Research, have for many years encouraged me to try new courses. Many ideas in this book emerged from my course, "Risking Change," and from "Female Friendship," co-taught at the New School with my best friend, Janet Wolfe. This book reflects what we learned from each other, and from class members, about the therapeutic importance of good quality female friendships as a natural resource for women.

In teaching "Becoming Your Independent Self" with Janice La Rouche, career counselor, I learned a great deal about the working woman and strategies for women in the job market.

Special thanks go to Phyllis Stern for her research work, suggestions, and willingness to transcribe tapes in a rush. And to Thomas Homsey, my secretary, for his suggestions, and cooperation in all sorts of ways in helping this book come to fruition. And also to my close friends who have all cheered me on in various ways. I particularly want to thank Phyllis Haynes, who helped open doors for me and who wouldn't let me get discouraged when the going was rough.

I also want to thank my daughter, Sylvia Russianoff, who along with her friends—especially Lisa Benson—kept me privy to the preadolescent and postadolescent problems I had long forgotten. And my heartfelt appreciation for Richard Levy, close friend and lawyer who piloted me through troubled waters listening with therapeutic ear to my frustrations while steadily keeping me on course; and for Carol Houck Smith, without whom this book would not have been written, because it was she who first urged me to put my thoughts in book form.

And a very, very special thank-you to Elin Schoen, whose superior writing talent, quick grasp of ideas, organizational ability, and unique perspective helped this book come into being; and also for introducing me to my agent, Wendy Weil, and to my editor, Gene Stone, whose enthusiasm and faith in the material made a dream become reality.

Contents

Introduction

This book is for just about every woman. The reason I say, "just about"—instead of going all the way and addressing all women—is that there *are* women out there who have no need of a man around the house (or elsewhere in their private lives) to make them feel complete. There *are* women who are completely autonomous, capable of being alone, even of living alone—and liking it.

But all too many women, as I have seen in my practice, in my classes at New York's New School for Social Research, and in my travels, feel that only a male presence in their lives can make their lives truly complete. This book is for them.

My purpose is not to knock the joys of love and the rewards of marriage or living with a man. I am happily married. I love men and feel that a good, solid, profound relationship with a man is something to which a woman might well aspire—but not to the exclusion of all else, not at the expense of her selfhood.

The purpose of this book is to help women find out what "all else" is (and it differs, of course, for every woman), to develop that "selfhood," to feel good about themselves as *people*, and to get the most out of their professional, social, and personal lives—without over-reliance on men as their mirrors and their mentors.

The women's movement has succeeded in improving women's lives in many areas and has inspired women to work harder at fulfilling their potential. But, while more and more women are functioning independently in jobs and careers and behaving more assertively—even aggressively—in all respects, many of them are still held back, to varying degrees, by the inner chant that tells them, "I am nothing without a man."

And it is, for the most part, an *inner* chant, something women don't like to admit.

"But I don't think I'm nothing without a man!" my stepdaughter said to me recently. "Well, not altogether, anyway."

Many patients tend to take this same position—initially, at least. And I have a feeling that if I made a cross-country tour, polling women of all ages on whether their definition of happiness *begins* with "having a good marriage" (or a reasonable facsimile thereof), the majority of women might say "No" (but think "Yes").

Nowadays, "housewife" is not a fashionable career option. Nor is it chic to admit that, on the whole, you'd rather land a man than a promotion.

The reason I am speaking of life choices in terms of fashion, as if they were skirt lengths or trouser shapes, is that our behavior and life-styles—or what we think our behavior and life-styles should be—are no less subject to majority rule, expert opinion, messages from the media, and group pressure than the clothes we wear.

But the truth is, despite all the fashionably liberated

rhetoric going around, most women do orient their lives to a very great extent around getting and then holding on to a mate—or, at least, a steady date. Often, when you delve beneath a fashionable declaration of independence, the picture is entirely different.

For example, a recent, front-page headline in *The New York Times* announced, "Many Young Women Now Say They'd Pick Family Over Career." The article, by Dena Kleiman, described the conflicts that female undergraduates at several East Coast colleges were facing: How to have a career, a husband, children—how to have "it all." If "it all" wasn't possible, quite a few of the young women interviewed were ready to sacrifice the job for the husband and children. The assumption seemed to be that, although a career may or may not be satisfying, the husband-and-children alternative would definitely be satisfying.

One senior at Princeton claimed that she was applying only to urban law schools, the better to meet men. Although she planned to spend time abroad after graduation, if the "right person should come along, it would be more important for me to spend time with him than running around Japan for six months."

In my own practice, I hear this sentiment echoed over and over from the women who come to me for "help" with either relationship problems or lack-of-a-relationship problems.

Lots of women expect me to help them work magical changes on their psyches, hoping that then they will be able to attract a man. A new hairdo, exquisite makeup, and a dress-for-success (but not the business kind) wardrobe wasn't the answer. So they think that maybe they need their psyches redone.

And when I suggest to women who are desperate to find a man that perhaps they *could* be happy even if they do not find one, I usually meet with great resistance. The notion strikes them as not only unappealing but also unrealistic, impossible, unbelievable!

"What's wrong with me?" my average patient wants to know. "Why aren't men beating down my door?" One patient begged me to transfer her from individual to group therapy—as long as it was a co-ed group! That way, you see, she'd get to look for that special someone even as she got her psyche in good enough shape to land him!

Of course, women aren't the only people who are overreliant on the opposite sex. Men are dependent, too. My male patients are often miserable over bad relationships (or having no relationships). I've consulted with enough bachelors to know that the carefree playboy is pretty much a myth. There are playboys, all right, but I've seldom met one who was totally free of the very same cares that plague single women.

These so-called "most wanted men" rush home from work and straight to the phone to make a date. God forbid they should spend the evening alone! And I've treated many a widower, anxious to get married to fill the unfaceable void in his life.

Many women envy men because they think men have more fun. It's easier, these women think, for men to be "swingers." But what women who think this way overlook is that men are often "swingers" not because they are expressing their lust for life or their lust, period, but because they hate being alone just as we do. "Swinging" is a cover-up. It helps in avoiding the void—at least temporarily.

Women and men are not as different from each other as we've all been led to believe—and this knowledge helps in kicking the whole dependency syndrome, as you'll see in later chapters.

But I've chosen to address myself to women in this book—for several reasons. First of all, although both men and women rely too much on the opposite sex for emotional sustenance, there are differences in the nature and degree of the dependency. Women's needs tend to seep into *all* areas of their lives. Men, after all, are programmed, as they always have been, that they must support themselves—and, usually, a family. They are more career-oriented than women. The work a man does is a source of pride, refuge, and self-esteem to him.

Women, for all their gains in the working world, still tend to get their refuge, self-esteem, and pride more from the home, the family, the man they landed.

Although a male politician, for instance, might choose to marry a woman who will be a political asset, he does not normally rely on the presence of this woman by his side to define him (politically or otherwise). All too many women, however, gain status in the world (and in their own eyes) via the man they marry. You get more status if you marry a neurosurgeon than if you marry a cabdriver. If the neurosurgeon is world famous, that's more status still.

Men don't, for the most part, resort to this means of acquiring an identity. For many men, having a famous or supersuccessful wife is, in fact, undesirable, because they find it threatening or demeaning.

So, while it is important for men to learn to be less dependent on women for emotional input, it is crucial, for the majority of women, to become less dependent on men. It is a matter of life or death, of having a fulfilled life or suffering the death of the spirit, a woman's true self, her identity.

The second reason that I am writing this book specifically for women is that women are way ahead of men in the area of seeking self-awareness. More women lead men to counselors or into therapy than the other way around. More women than men read "self-help" books. In fact, there are more self-help books written for women than for men. Bookstores have "Women's Studies" sections—not "Men's Studies." Women's magazines are more numerous than men's, and their orientation is more therapeutic.

And in most male-female relationships, the woman is the pioneer of the joint psyche. Women do more tending to relationships, more shaping of the logistics of relationship-maintenance. Women cater, bend, manipulate, adjust, do research. They're more adaptable than men.

Also, women have a movement behind them. And the feminist movement translates into a multitude of organizations that exist for the purpose of women supporting other women, and womanhood in general, politically and psychologically.

So if *people* are going to become less dependent on

A Relationship as the mainstay of a happy life, it is women who will lead the way.

Now for the third, and most important, reason I've chosen to address myself to women in this book: Many more women than men end up living alone.

In New York City, according to a recent *New York Times* study, there are a million more women "of marriageable age" than men. In the country at large, according to 1979 government statistics, there were 14.6 million older women (over 65) and 10 million older men.

In a recent *New York Times* article about the White House Mini-Conference on Older Women, Judy Klemesrud summed up other sobering statistics: "More than one out of two women in the United States can expect to be a widow at the age of 65 or over. . . . Chances of remarriage for an older woman are slim; after the age of 65, widowers are nine times as likely to remarry as widows. . . . One out of every four women working today can expect to be poor in her old age. . . . Over and over again in informal sessions, female delegates to the conference kept using the word invisible when describing their status."

There is no way to estimate exactly how many women in this country will experience living without a man at some time in their lives—but the percentage would be surprisingly high.

It is vital, therefore, that women of all ages, single and married, realize that living without a man does not automatically mean that their lives must be luster-less, that they must be lonely and miserable.

There is a moment in *Possessed*, the classic film portrait of a woman who goes berserk because the man she loves does not love her back, where Joan Crawford is nagging Van Heflin (the unfortunate object of her obsession). He wants to work. She wants attention. He looks up from his papers and says something like this: "Why is it, the minute a man gets interested in his work, that a woman has to try to get him to show interest in her?"

That was in the 1940s. No film maker today would dare include a line like that in a movie—unless it was facetious. Women today have supposedly gotten over that girlish, simpering, clinging-vine stuff. Women today have supposedly shed "traditional female behavior." Supposedly.

In real life, meanwhile, most of my female patients—today—would identify instantly with poor Joan Crawford in *Possessed*. And every man I know—today—would understand what Van Heflin meant.

Women have, indeed, come a long way—socially, sexually, and, to a lesser extent, economically. Emotionally, however, they still have a long way to go. This book is a first step.

Why Do I Think I Am Nothing Without a Man?

I
Desperate Dependence: A Definition

About 95 percent of my female patients think that they are nothing without a man. But this is not something they tell me immediately.

Usually, the first complaint I hear is "Why do I feel so empty so much of the time?" Or "Why, since I have a good job, lots of hobbies, and wonderful friends, do I feel so unfulfilled?" Or even: "Now that I've made it to the directorship of —— Corp., I find it a hollow victory. That is, I'm successful! I've arrived! But I still feel . . . hollow, like something's missing."

My patients ultimately confess what is missing, too. They tell me: "If I had a man around, I'd no longer feel empty and unfulfilled." Or, in the case of a woman who does have a man around: "If he spent more time with me, I'd no longer feel that something's missing."

There are plenty of variations on these themes, of course. But you get the idea. Problem: the blahs. Solution: true love and modern romance.

One of my new patients—I'll call her Molly—informed me during her first session that if she had some wonderful man in her life right now (she's recently divorced), she wouldn't feel the need to go into therapy at all. Molly is an outstanding young actress who has appeared in several television movies and, at the time she began therapy, had just won rave reviews in a supporting role on Broadway.

Yet Molly was unhappy because she did not have a leading man offstage. I asked her what I ask all women who feel that a man is the missing link, the cure for what ails them: "What if you had to live your whole life without a man?"

And Molly responded typically: "I couldn't. It's unimaginable. I'd just be depressed all the time—because I need love. I need someone to talk to, someone who's mine, who cares about me to the exclusion of all other women. I think this is the most important thing in life, not only for me but for every woman I know. I suppose my life wouldn't end if I never got married again or if I never had a serious love affair. But I wouldn't enjoy it too much. I'm not enjoying it now."

Upon further questioning, Molly admitted that she does get *some* enjoyment from life. But she can't shake that feeling of being, somehow, incomplete—like a jigsaw puzzle with a piece missing. She explained that the reason she is not totally unhappy, twenty-four hours a day, is that she has hope. She considers her single state strictly temporary. "I'll meet someone," she told me, "and then everything will be okay."

In other words, Molly was telling me that she thinks, deep inside, that she is nothing without a man.

Brenda admitted the same thing—and just as circuitously. But Brenda, an architect, does have a man in her life—Josh. Brenda didn't have to tell me how successful she is; I had read a magazine article about her. But the Brenda who showed up in my office was not the confident sophisticate depicted in the article.

"I don't know what's happened to me since my marriage," Brenda said. "I used to go off on assignments to the other side of the world without even thinking about it. Now I try to get out of such projects. I want local ones. I'm just not happy unless I'm with Josh. If he can't go to a party and I go alone, I don't have fun. So I'd rather just stay home. And, you know, we just got a new car. It's a sports car, and I can't drive stick—so I just let Josh drive us everywhere. And the worst thing is, we could afford another car—one I could drive—but I don't even want one. I *like* being chauffeured. I like it, but at the same time I resent this . . . this *symbol* of my self-induced bondage."

As Brenda's dilemma suggests, you don't have to live alone to think that you are nothing without a man. You don't have to be divorced or widowed or never married. You can be living with a man or married and think that without this man you would be lonely, socially inhibited, emotionally and sexually barren.

I've counseled numbers of married women who absolutely had no lives of their own because their hopes and dreams and plans and daily routines revolved so tightly around those of the men with whom they lived.

Thinking that you are nothing without a man is a problem women share regardless of marital status—and also regardless of age, nationality, income, upbringing, professional standing, religion, and personal appearance.

The enormous desire for a male partner is probably the closest thing to a common denominator that women have. As one of my patients once said, "You're damned if you do and damned if you don't. If you have a man, you feel you can't live without him. If you don't have one, you feel like you can't start living till you get one. We're all in the same boat."

Each of us can get off the boat. But before we discuss solutions, we have to understand a little bit more about the problem.

When I say that thinking you are nothing without a man is a problem, I do not mean to imply that dependence on another human being who happens to be male is, in itself, negative. Nor do I mean to suggest that living alone is the best of all possible ways to live—although there are women who choose to be alone rather than settle for just any man. And that is all to the good.

But human beings do crave companionship. They are innately dependent. John Donne wrote, "No man is an island, entire of itself." Well, no woman is, either. And it is blissful for a woman and a man to live together, sharing their thoughts and experiences, expressing love for each other physically and verbally—and, yes, depending on each other in many ways.

This is natural, desirable, satisfying, altogether wonderful.

It is not, however, the only recipe for happiness in human experience.

Nor does it necessarily imply that the female partner in this successful collaboration thinks that she is nothing without a man.

Being dependent on others in various ways, and having others depend on you, is an important and very pleasant part of the dynamics of normal human experience. But being *too* dependent, and especially being overly dependent on one male person, is another matter entirely.

Desperate dependence, which is how I characterize that sort of void-without-a-man feeling, that clinging behavior I find in so many of my patients, invades every aspect of your life and inhibits you from living it to the fullest. Desperate dependence may sound melodramatic. But it does not always connote the psychological equivalent of drowning in high waters and praying for someone—a male someone—to jump in and save you.

Desperate dependence also refers to any woman for whom the major focus in life is a man, or the lack of one, a woman who feels adrift or on the prowl, or one who feels that the world views her as abnormal without a male consort, one who feels listless and purposeless when "her" man is out of town, at work, or, anyway, not right there with her.

There are degrees of desperate dependence, but the consequences are always the same: By allowing the male connection to supersede all other sources of pleasure, fulfillment, entertainment, and reward in your life, you are perpetually the damsel in distress waiting for him to rescue you from loneliness, confusion, emptiness, boredom.

The desperately dependent woman pivots, or longs to pivot, around a person outside herself, a man who loves her. In the Romeo and Juliet scheme of things, to which so many of my patients subscribe, the man must pivot around the woman, too. That is, he, too, must be desperately dependent. Molly used a very telling phrase when describing what having a man around meant to her. She said she wants "someone who's mine, who cares about me to the exclusion of all other women."

She wants him to be totally absorbed in her. She wants him to have an all-consuming need for her. Molly is very much under the Romeo and Juliet spell—not that she would go all the way and expect her lover to annihilate himself over her lifeless body (should her demise precede his). Not that she would consider literally following her lover to his grave.

Few women take Romeo and Juliet *that* seriously. Yet the Romeo and Juliet ideal, expressed in our marriage vows, enshrined in our fantasies, can permeate a woman's subconscious to the point that, in her marriage, she and her husband are "the whole world to each other." They always walk and sit hand in hand. They brag about never having spent more than five minutes at a stretch without each other in their umpteen years of marriage.

"How beautiful," Molly said, when I described such a relationship. "How ideal!"

But in idealizing such a couple, Molly did not consider what might happen when one of them dies and the other literally cannot survive alone, never having learned to stand on her—or his—own two feet.

This inability to go on is seldom manifest in anything so dramatic as the final scene of *Romeo and Juliet*—but I have seen widows, and widowers, literally fade away. I watched this happen to my mother. After my father died, she said, "I can't live without him." And, sure enough, she died soon afterward of leukemia, which I have often thought might have been psychosomatically induced.

And I have seen patients of mine, following the death or departure of a husband or lover on whom they were desperately dependent, become joyless, self-pitying, motivationless, even self-destructive—which, to me, adds up to living suicide, killing everything about yourself and within yourself except your physical being.

So—while the Romeo and Juliet story is very romantic, emulating it in your own life, however inadvertently, however loosely, is not in your own best interests.

And it is my goal in this book to encourage all those who are under the Romeo and Juliet spell to substitute for this romantic ideal, which is not so ideal, a healthy, life-enhancing reality: to stop pivoting around a man as your core of security and to learn to pivot around the core of security that you build up within yourself—and to learn that you do not need a man by your side in order to feel beautiful, worthwhile, loveable, smart, confident, joyous, and whole.

I want you to imagine this inner core of security as I see it: It's like having a second backbone. It's a solid spine of confidence that is part of you; you take it with you wherever you go. And with this inner source of sustenance, you do not have to rely for safe harbor or for self-esteem on anyone outside of yourself.

But having this second backbone does not isolate you from the man in your life. It does not make you less desirable to men. Rather, it makes you more desirable. And it enables you to enjoy a man in a much richer way than you do if you are desperately dependent on him.

To pivot around your own inner core of security is a realistic goal. It, unlike variations on the romantic ideal, is within every woman's grasp.

Now, I am well aware that we're constantly being bombarded by today's culture telling us how much we need a man, that unless we establish a love nest, set up housekeeping with a man, we're not living out our true destinies. And the feeling that "I am not complete without a man by my side" is a reaction to innumerable cultural cues (which we'll examine in Chapter II). Society's programming causes women to be pliable, eager to mold and shape and adapt themselves to men and their interests.

Many people, men and women, regard this pliancy, this conformity, as the normal female condition. But it is, rather, the norm for women. And embodying the norm, in this case, is not constructive. Because pliancy can be a self-effacing trait. In being too adaptable, too flexible, a woman gives up a great deal of herself, gives up the right to define herself.

A woman whose behavior indicates that she desperately needs a man—even if she says to herself, "I am *not* desperate"—abdicates the right to be herself in any number of ways.

But there are any number of ways for her to win back this right. I feel very strongly that nearly any woman can break out of her cultural conditioning and become undependent.

Notice that I did not say "independent." Independence, to me, is simply a way of behaving. I've known countless women who act and speak independently— and yet they were still emotionally fixated on men.

So I prefer to use my own neologism—undependence—when referring to what this book is all about, getting unfixated on men, being as liberated emotionally as you are in other ways.

I have seen quite a few of my patients become undependent. And it has happened to me. My husband and I share a life that is full of collaboration and mutual enjoyment on every level that you can imagine. Yet we are each autonomous, very much involved in our individual careers, often content to pursue our individual interests alone, even if it means a long, physical separation.

When I mention my own undependent relationship to my patients, they are often dubious: "You mean that your involvement with your husband, your deep love for him, doesn't take precedence over other areas of your life? Let's say he's late getting home. You mean you never just sort of putter around till he gets there, killing time when you might have ninety-nine crucial things to do, feeling insecure not necessarily because you think he might be unfaithful but just because *he's not there?*"

The fact is, I don't have those feelings anymore. But I certainly did at one time. I identified strongly, if in retrospect, to a portion of a friend's diary in which she described the phenomenon she calls "window sitting."

One night, as she perched on her windowsill, as usual, waiting for her sporadically late lover, she decided to take notes on what was going through her mind:

> I'm only sitting here through one more commercial from the TV I've got my back on. One more commercial's worth of window sitting. One more plug for Lenny's Clam Bar in Queens.
>
> I will wait for one more cab to stop in front of the building and then I am going to sleep. Or I'll read. Or something.
>
> I could sit here at the window and remember nice things about my childhood or this morning. Or I could work. But this occasion, this waiting game, is too holy to smear with diverting thoughts or constructive deeds. I don't want to come off my limb. I like it here in limbo.
>
> Aha . . . a cab is stopping out front. It must be him. Who else could it be at this hour? The fat French seamstress who lives on the fourteenth floor and her fat poodle, that's who. They each limp to the same beat: Boom-chacha, boom-chacha!

10 ▫

This is absolutely the last herd of cabs I'm monitoring. This is absolutely the last time I'm ever going to indulge in this mindless waiting game. Tomorrow I'll be normal.

Or maybe this is normal? Or maybe it's become normal for me? Everyone has their own normality. For a junkie, shooting junk is normal. Some people have a normal temperature of 96.2. Some people put salted peanuts in Pepsi and think it's delicious. And normal.

Maybe for me, stupidity is normal. Because, let's face it, smart people don't dangle their torsos out 15th floor windows in 20 degree weather. Smart people say, "Screw this," and go to sleep.

Another round of traffic. *Where the hell is he?*

I have done some window sitting in my time. And I've indulged in related nonactivities that, for many women, are a favorite form of home-entertainment. I'm quite familiar with the following nonproductive, even counterproductive pursuits—which are, besides window sitting, primary symptoms of thinking you are nothing without a man:

1. **Method Acting:** You may be willing to fritter away the entire evening window sitting, but at least part of that time is spent setting up your welcome-home scenario so he should never know you've been window sitting.

Therefore, window sitting becomes constructive in one sense: You see him coming. This gives you time to rush into position before he comes through the door. He will, therefore, find you:

Immersed in a fragrant bubblebath

Busily doing your nails

Asleep, with a fallen book (something along the lines of *Being & Nothingness*) on your chest

Giggling into the phone, then telling the dial tone, "Oh! Here he is! Gotta go!"

Behind the locked bathroom door picking your cuticles or staring at the wall. But from his vantage point, it seems as if you're in there tending to important business, such as making yourself beautiful—for him.

2. **Plotting Revenge:** This consists, typically, of spending the evening making ultimatums.

You are reading a book, for instance, but instead of focusing on the printed word, you're promising yourself that "If he doesn't get here before page thirty, I'm spending the night at Mary's! I won't even leave a note! Let him worry about where *I* am for a change!"

Another popular form of revenge is taking the phone off the hook, or, not answering it. Should he call, therefore, he'll know you're far too preoccupied to be worrying about whether he'll call—or arrive, for that matter. Should he call repeatedly, he might actually get worried about you—which serves him right!

3. **Wine and Song:** Everyone has her own personal soundtrack, the songs that bring back memories, music to weep by. A little wine helps, too. By playing your songs and drinking far into the night, you can milk your anxious anticipation for all it's worth.

What fascinates me about all these nonactivities is that women actually enjoy them. I know I did. And my window sitting friend came right out and admitted, "I like it here in limbo." Her account of window sitting sounds as if she's off to one side, watching herself suffer. And it seems so romantic, pining and mooning or plotting revenge or planning scenarios. All you need is a feather fan and a boa-trimmed peignoir. It's a form of self-indulgence, all this romantic suffering in the name of love, all this carefully staged, self-enforced drama constructed around waiting for his arrival.

Only his arrival, the moment you're waiting for, will allow you to feel worthwhile, enthusiastic, purposeful, appreciated—alive again.

But when he's there, another set of symptoms of desperate dependence tend to swing into action. Sometimes, his mere presence isn't enough. You still don't feel worthwhile, enthusiastic, purposeful, appreciated, alive again. So you might resort to behavior calculated to encourage him to bolster your sagging self-image:

1. **Twenty Questions:** This is the most direct means of seeking reassurance. The questions go more or less like this:

"Do you love me?"

"Do you still love me?"

"Do you love me as much as when we first met?"

"If there were a fire, would you rescue me first? Or your files?"

"Why do you love me, exactly?"

"Would you still love me if I were old and wrinkled?"

"Would you still love me if I were in an automobile accident and got scarred for life?"

"Do I still turn you on as much as I did when we first met?"

"Do I turn you on more than *she* did?" (Meaning his ex-wife or ex-girlfriend)

"Am I pretty?"

"Do I look okay?"

"Do you think I look fat?"

"Am I as pretty as *she* is?" (Meaning his ex-wife, his ex-girlfriend, or some woman on the other side of the room)

"Am I good in bed?"

"Am I better in bed than any woman you've ever been with?"

"D'you like the rack of lamb?" (or whatever you spend the day cooking for him)

"D'you think I should get a nose job?"

"Would you still love me if I went to work/quit my job?"

"Do you think anybody in the world's ever been as much in love as we are?"

"If I died/left you, what would you do?" (The hoped-for answer: "I would curl up and die")

2. **The Baiting Game:** In which you tell him you love him solely so that he will say, "I love you, too."

3. **The Compliments Game:** In which you build up his ego so that he will appreciate, even more, your presence in his life. You shower him with compliments, usually outrageous:

"You're the handsomest man I ever saw!"

"Next to you, Robert Redford's a real washout!"

"Your body reminds me of Michelangelo's *David*." You are hoping to be rewarded, of course, not only by his renewed appreciation of you but by similar compliments from him.

4. **Mea Culpa:** Confessing your faults-of-the-moment is a more subtle form of provoking a reassuring response than direct questioning. Statements of fact (or fancy) such as the following are intended to elicit a fond "Are you crazy?" reaction from a man, preferably accompanied by an affectionate glance or gestures that mean, "I would love you no matter what."

"Oh dear! I got a wrinkle next to my mouth—only on one side of my mouth, but . . ."

"If only I weren't so inept at bridge. I really mess up your game."

5. **The Inquisition:** "Why didn't you call if you knew you were gonna be three hours late?"

"Who else was at the meeting?"

"If it was a *business* meeting, in the *office*, then how come you couldn't get to a phone?"

6. **Calculated Hypochondria:** You're as healthy as a horse. Yet you may feign illness in order to get his attention or to make him feel guilty because he was late, didn't call, hasn't said "I love you" for three whole days, etc.

Do any of these scenarios sound familiar?

He's late. He arrives home and discovers you sprawled on the couch. You look up at him from under heavy eyelids. "I don't know what's wrong with me," you rasp. "I almost fainted before—and I'm still nauseous. But I feel better now that you're here . . ."

He calls from the office to say he's going to be late. "Oh, well, that's okay," you tell him. "I'll call my brother. He can take me to the hospital. Oh, nothing. Just a fever—104."

He hasn't been affectionate enough lately. "Darling," you whisper as he drifts off to sleep. "I can't breathe right." He is alarmed and wants to call a doctor. "No, no," you whisper, "just—hold me."

7. **Public Relations:** You refuse to circulate more than two feet away from him at a party.

You act less intelligent than you are in order to make him feel more brilliant—maybe even more brilliant than he is.

You insist on hand holding, lap sitting, hugging, etc., in public—even if this makes him feel uncomfortable. ("He'll get used to it," you think. "He'll get to like it.")

You insist that he return your physical tokens of affection in public—or become paranoid if he does not do so automatically.

You get the bends if he asks another woman to dance.

You insist on going with him on his social/business outings and then sit there, bored, but *with him*—when your time would be spent more productively doing your own work or doing something you enjoy with your own friends.

You accompany him to: a movie that he wants to see and you don't. Or a sports activity that he likes and you don't like. Or a trip to the hardware store to shop for his tools. (You couldn't care less about his tools).

You hover while he's washing the car/fixing the broken lamp/making a phone call that doesn't concern you.

Think of all the energy that goes into this all-consuming focus on a man! Think of all the woman-hours wasted, time that could have been spent creating something, learning, accomplishing. Many of my female patients have complained to me that "There aren't enough hours in a day." Or "I never get time to myself." Or "I haven't read a serious book since college."

No wonder! It's difficult to pursue your career, hobbies, etc. when you're so busy pursuing him. It's difficult to tend to your intellectual or creative growth when you're so preoccupied with gorging yourself on the emotional level. It's difficult to develop your innate skills and your own interests when desperate dependence keeps you so beholden to a man that you've lost track of what your skills and interests are!

And desperate dependence does become an enormous obstacle to self-knowledge and self-growth because it not only manifests itself in the isolated symptoms I've enumerated, but it can seep into your entire life-style, determining not only the nature of your relationship with a man but your choice of the man with whom you have a relationship.

Let me tell you about one of the most extreme cases of desperate dependence I've ever encountered. This was one of my first patients. She was married to a paraplegic who had no use whatsoever of his lower limbs. She was completely devoted to him, hovered over him, saw to his every need.

And, as time went on, he spent more and more time at home and needed a nurse to manage some of the details of his life. His wife—my patient—was working to support them. She would call home several times a day to check on him; she built her whole life around servicing him and taking care of him.

And one day she came home from work and found that he wasn't there. He had left a note, saying that he had fallen in love with the nurse and that he wanted a divorce as soon as possible. My patient was devastated.

My feeling was that she had been so clinging in the course of waiting on this man that she also became boring to him. And she did, in fact, tell me that she was shocked that he'd run off with the nurse because he told her all the time how angry the nurse made him, how she teased him and wouldn't give him his juice with his pill. But in the final analysis, he found the slightly recalcitrant nurse more fun to be with than his slavishly devoted wife.

And the wife was flabbergasted. She couldn't figure out what had gone wrong. Since she had married him feeling, at least subconsciously, that "Since he can't walk, he'll never run away from me," she felt secure in her marriage. She really loved and admired her husband. He was a knowledgeable man, good-looking, witty. And she felt thrilled that she had him. And that's how she put it—that she *had* him, like a possession.

But she derived her security from the fact that he was crippled. This made her feel "safe."

Another way to feel "safe," according to my professional encounters, is to "buy" a man. I'm always surprised by the growing number of wealthy and successful women who feel that if they can make a man dependent on money that they either inherited or earn, then the man won't ever want to leave.

Supporting a man can be an act of love, of course; the flip side of the traditional setup in which the man supports the woman.

But sometimes, supporting a man is an act of overdependence. Sometimes, it is motivated not only, or not so much, by love as by a fear of losing him. Some women I've seen in my practice feel, deep down inside, that being the breadwinner is unfeminine. But they feel that *totally* supporting a man does not threaten their femininity—at least, this is the subconscious rationale—because serving a man, which is what total support adds up to, is very feminine.

I'm thinking of one of my patients in particular. I'll call her Rosemary. Rosemary, an account executive with a major advertising agency, married a very good-looking television technician whom I'll call Lloyd.

Lloyd, an intelligent man who was, nevertheless, too insecure to hustle and promote himself, fell easily into the role of "inspiring" Rosemary to promote herself, to be more creative, to make more money. Meanwhile, Lloyd quit his job to become a freelance technician. The net result of that move was that he was not working much of the time. Rosemary encouraged him to write scripts and to develop his own potential and talent while she underwrote his career. At one point, Rosemary decided as a surprise to put $100,000 in Lloyd's bank account. Lloyd promptly bought himself a lot of clothes and somehow ended up working even less than he had been.

Lloyd and Rosemary both rationalized that, without Lloyd, Rosemary couldn't possibly have been so successful. They both rationalized that Lloyd was an inspiration to her. And the fact that Lloyd kept the home fires burning, doing numerous househusband tasks, was further justification to Rosemary that their life together was ideal.

Rosemary, despite her professional achievements, was quite insecure and did not think that she could "hook" another man. She thought men, on the whole, were hostile to supersuccessful women. She had decided, a long time ago, first unconsciously, then consciously, that the only way she could hope to have the security of a home and the love of a man, was to find a man who needed her financially, as well as in other ways, and give him a life-style too comfortable to leave.

As for the tradition of women being supported by men—although increasing numbers of women are contributing financially to their households, I still see an amazing number of women in my practice who could have stepped right out of Maribel Morgan's book, *The Total Woman*.

But I feel Morgan's recipe for bliss—namely, vamping and creative seduction, carried out in the interests of keeping that man in tow—simply doesn't work. Total devotion to your man is not the road to inner fulfillment.

A case in point is Audrey, who at forty-five was bored, depressed, and felt that her life was empty and that she was a failure—or at least, that she was not the success she wanted to be in terms of her marriage. And she definitely only thought of success in terms of marriage.

Audrey is married to Joe, a successful city planner. Audrey takes lots of courses and studies painting. She belongs to various clubs, the main purpose of which seems to be fund-raising for various causes.

One of the many things that worried Audrey was that Joe was spending more and more time at the office. He was deeply wrapped up in his business. He was almost always late coming home and often spent the night in his office.

I asked Audrey on her first visit if she suspected that Joe might have been having an affair, since she indicated that she thought he had lost interest in her—a situation that terrified Audrey, who had grown up with the understanding that it is always a good idea to make love frequently with your husband so that he won't look elsewhere for sex.

Audrey told me she was quite sure that Joe was not having an affair with anyone else. "He's a good husband. I know he cares about me," she said. "He's just very preoccupied with his work."

Audrey worked very hard herself. She kept the house clean and neat. She read the newspaper every day and thought up interesting topics to introduce at the dinner table on those occasions when Joe was home for dinner. She spent time each day at the health club where she exercised, took saunas, worked at staying slim and lithe.

To Audrey, the idea of losing Joe was a nightmare. She could not face this possibility. But she felt she was running out of ideas to keep him tuned in on her. She had decided that Joe was a genius who really was more interested in his work than anything else. And she wanted only to be the supportive woman behind the scenes, pleading with him, cajoling him, never complaining, smiling all the time, and always greeting him at the door with his martini in her hand.

In addition to spending time at the health club, Audrey spent time on her nails, her hair, and her face. She had heard Joe comment about attractive young women from time to time. She felt that in order to keep him interested in her, she had to appear as young as she could.

Audrey liked to go on conventions with her husband. She looked forward to the several vacations they took during the year. But Joe had recently been trying to talk her out of going to conventions because, he told her, "There's nothing for you to do. And you spend most of your time alone anyway, sitting around waiting for me."

Audrey protested: "But I enjoy waiting for you. I really don't want to stay home and just miss you."

Eventually, Joe told Audrey that he wanted to have a marriage of convenience. He would give her whatever money she needed, take care of her expenses. He urged her to travel. He said he'd pay for whatever trips she wanted to take. But he told her point-blank that he was involved with two other women. He found them fascinating. Both of them were city planners. He wanted to spend more time with both of these women, taking them on trips with him. He felt his relationship with Audrey was over, other than his responsibility to maintain her in the manner to which she was accustomed. He didn't particularly want a divorce, because he had no desire to remarry. But if Audrey wanted a divorce, he would give her one.

Audrey felt that her life was over. Her "ideal" behavior—always being at her husband's beck and call, trying to create a joyful atmosphere for him to come home to, even when she was tired or depressed—had been rewarded with utter rejection.

Audrey's situation is hardly unusual as she is actually a composite of many women I've seen. She represents a syndrome which many therapists consider the most standard type of case that they encounter in their woman patients. Audrey typifies women who, having devoted their lives to being what a man wanted, find themselves without the man and at a loss as to what to do with their lives.

The Total Woman, from what I've seen, usually feels—or ends up feeling—anything but total. *Totaled* is more like it.

And you don't have to be a housewife to be a Total Woman. I've met many a Total Woman with a job. The job is merely an appendage to her life, which still revolves around a man.

Anne, for instance, cringes with guilt if she is late coming home from work. She "understands," on the other hand, if her husband is late. That, to her, is a male prerogative.

Her husband, for his part, certainly appreciates the extra income her job brings in. He tolerates her working—"as long as dinner's on the table when I get home."

Anne feels that she really shouldn't be working, and that she certainly shouldn't enjoy it. She went to work not so much because current social thinking pressured her into believing that being a housewife wasn't enough, but because of economic pressure. She and her husband couldn't make ends meet on his salary.

But there is no question in Anne's mind that she would drop her job in a moment to follow her husband to another location, should he find a better position, even if there was no opportunity for her to use whatever talents she has developed at this new location. She would make such a change at the drop of a hat and feel that it was her "duty."

The Total Woman with a job, like the housebound Total Woman, spends an inordinate amount of time primping to please her husband, keeping the house spic 'n span, meal planning. And, of course, she has primary child-raising responsibilities.

The curious thing is that even when the husband offers to help out, or actually helps out, on the home front, as Anne's husband has been known to do, the woman herself makes it clear that the home is her turf. Anne feels guilty if she slacks off at home. She suffers from the Superwoman complex, as many women do. She wants to live up to the image made famous in the Enjoli perfume commercial, in which the glamorous model actually splits into three separate personae as she torch-sings: "I can bring home the bacon, cook it up in the pan—and never, never let him forget he's a man. Cause I'm a wo-man, W-O-M-A-N . . ."

Another patient of mine, another aspiring Super-woman, exhibits an interesting inner conflict of interests that I see frequently in women. Her husband, untouched by the feminist propaganda that she reads to him from the magazines or that comes up in conversations with the couples with whom they socialize, expects her to do all the "right," wifely things.

Ellen sabotages her efforts to "reform" him because, deep inside, she believes that a man's place is really not in the kitchen. Intellectually, she knows it's unfair for her to work and also do the housework, including cooking, entertaining, grocery shopping, making sure the family doesn't run out of toothpaste and toilet paper, getting the clothes to the laundry—while her husband merely works.

But Ellen, on the emotional level, *wants* to please her man through all the millions of life-style-maintenance tasks that she now thinks are drudgery.

So she stands in the kitchen, concocting a man-pleasing dinner, for instance, and seething with resentment—hating him for not helping her, hating herself for not insisting that he help her, and, at the same time, realizing that she doesn't really want him to help her.

"It's so gratifying," she says, "to hear his murmurs of appreciation over the dinner. And really, I love to cook—and he doesn't. So it makes sense for me to do it."

It happens that many women truly do love to cook. But, as it turns out, Ellen only enjoys cooking gourmet meals for guests and not the nightly meat 'n potatoes regime her husband prefers. It's not that she loves to cook so much as she is programmed to think she should love to cook. And, most of all, she loves her husband's pleasure in her cooking.

There is nothing wrong with that, of course—if you are unconflicted and content in your relationship. But Ellen is terribly conflicted and not at all content.

Ellen regards her job very much like Anne does. She says things such as, "Gee, it's great to get out of the house, to make my own money. . . ." But she actually merely goes through the motions on the job. Neither of these women are in dead-end jobs, either. They could move up. But they won't let themselves.

Interestingly, some of the most overly assertive, ambitious career women I've met, women who might be called "tough" on the job, are entirely the opposite on the home front. Their co-workers wouldn't recognize them.

I've met quite a few Closet Clinging Vines, as I call them, women who are high-powered dynamos at work but absolutely infantile with men. Lucy, for example, is the manager of several supermarkets. She handles her job extraordinarily well and runs a tight ship. She pressures the vendors to deliver, returns inadequate merchandise, insists on instant compensation for the damaged goods. She's adamant about employees' being on time, not smoking on the job, sticking to all the rules.

26 □

Lucy told me once that she overheard two clerks discussing her. One called her "that ball breaker." Lucy was not displeased. She wants to be known for ruling with an iron hand—on the job.

Every evening, however, Lucy makes a dash for home where she slips into "something more comfortable"; jeans or, frequently, a sexy robe. Then she starts dinner. Before long, she is turning to Ray, her husband, with her big blue eyes and looking wistfully into space, asking him to please unscrew the top of a bottle. "I guess I'm just not strong enough," she explains.

Ray runs a construction company. He's an ex-football player. He adores his wife. Her petiteness makes him feel even taller than his six-foot-two. He calls Lucy his "little doll." He likes to pick her up to kiss her, leaving her a foot and a half off the ground.

Lucy regresses to babyhood when she is around Ray. She crawls in his lap, wanting to be cuddled. She asks his advice about everything. Although she makes important decisions at her supermarkets all day, at home she lets Ray make the decisions, about buying a car, about disciplining their two small children.

And Lucy is completely aware of her dual personality. She is far from dumb. She and Ray often laugh about what Lucy's employees would think to see her clinging to him at home. Lucy likes Ray's strong, bossy attitude with her. She says it makes her feel secure.

Lucy and Ray will probably continue their relationship as long as Ray feels good with her clinging to him, pampering him, worshipping him, and as long as Lucy is comfortable playing Ray's little girl.

It must be clear by now that the idea that true love and modern romance can cure general *malaise* is a fallacy. This idea is, in fact, itself a major cause of *malaise*.

If you don't have a man, you operate (or put off operating) on the premise that when you get one, you'll be and do and have everything you dream of being and doing and having. You postpone genuine enjoyment of work and play. You do not make life-commitments—such as deciding where you want to live permanently or buying real estate or establishing any kind of roots. Because you have made everything contingent on the man you're going to have. He will not only help you make it through the night; he will determine your daily routine and even your life-style.

If you are married or living with someone, chances are that you still don't escape the role of lady-in-waiting. Still, your enjoyment of life depends on the presence of a man. The only difference is that you now know who he is.

I find it sad that so many women spend so much of their lives on hold—waiting for Mr. Right to come along, waiting for him to come home, waiting for him to make them feel complete—instead of allowing themselves to be who they are, to emerge as themselves, to give themselves the right to enjoy, to feel complete in themselves.

I find it sad—and unnecessary—not that there are so many unmarried women in the world, but that there are so many *unfinished* women.

If you feel that you are one of these women, and if you want to complete yourself, you are in for an exhilarating adventure.

Becoming undependent, pivoting around your own inner core of security, means that:

1. Your career can flourish as never before—because you'll have more time and energy to invest in work.

2. Sex will be more satisfying psychologically and, therefore, physically.

3. You will forget what it means to be bored.

4. Your curiosity quotient will rise—and, with it, your options for excitement and enjoyment.

5. Your existing friendships will be far more rewarding.

6. You will make new friends more easily.

7. Loneliness will become a thing of the past—because you will actually relish those times when you are alone.

8. Aging will no longer loom as a formidable threat to your well-being.

9. You will look more attractive. (Your mind can do as much for your face as any cream or lotion.)

10. You may discover abilities you never suspected you had.

11. If you are married or living with a man, your relationship will improve and flourish.

12. If you are single, divorced, or widowed, your chances for establishing a wonderful relationship—not just any old relationship—with a man will be greater.

One thing that I cannot promise you is that becoming undependent will be an overnight or a simple process. After all, you didn't acquire your present world view or self-image overnight, did you?

I do not believe in formula cures: "Since you're X, you should do Y to become Z."

But I do have a methodology for getting over desperate dependence. It has worked for a great number of my patients. It can work for you.

It begins with understanding, thoroughly, how you became the person you are right now.

II

"How Did I Get This Way?"

A great number of my patients who think they are nothing without a man also believe that this condition is predestined.

Many women seem to feel virtually cast into the mold of desperate dependence. So it is understandable that the syndrome should appear to them as God's will or woman's fate. Certainly, passivity is—and always has been—a component of the traditional female image, a classic trait of femininity. There are numerous references to this compliance allegedly built into female nature in the annals of philosophy and literature.

One description that particularly rankles is Arthur Schopenhauer's essay "Of Women," which concludes:

> That woman is by nature meant to obey may be seen by the fact that the woman who is placed in the unnatural position of complete indepen-

dence immediately attaches herself to some man. Finally, she allows herself to be guided and ruled. It is because she needs a lord and master. If she is young, it will be a lover; if she is old, a priest.

What Schopenhauer arbitrarily consigned to female "nature" (according to his observations of women's behavior) has been attributed, by widely respected psychological theoreticians, to the female anatomy.

I have found, in my conversations with patients and with my colleagues, that there is a widespread adherence to the "empty vessel" explanation of female dependence which depicts women as actually being in a biological trap, psychologically programmed by their physical structure.

Helene Deutsch wrote, in her *Psychology of Women*:

> . . . the anatomy of the sex organs leaves no doubt as to the character of their aims: the masculine organ is made for active penetration, the feminine for passive reception. . . . The awakening of the vagina to full sexual functioning is entirely dependent upon the man's activity; and this absence of spontaneous vaginal activity constitutes the physiological background of feminine passivity.

According to Erik Erikson (in *Identity, Youth and Crisis*):

> . . . clinical observation suggests that in female experience an "inner space" is at the center of

despair even as it is at the very center of potential
fulfillment. Emptiness is the female form of per-
dition. . . . To be left, for her, means to be left
empty, to be drained of the blood of the body, the
warmth of the heart, the sap of life. . . . Am I
saying, then, that "anatomy is destiny?" Yes, it is
destiny, insofar as it determines not only the
range and configuration of physiological functioning and its limitation but also, to an extent,
personality configurations. The basic modalities
of woman's commitment and involvement naturally also reflect the ground plan of her body.

There is a compelling tidiness to this point of view.
It makes sense—but then so does the opposite way of
looking at biological destiny: Given that men pene-
trate and women receive, shouldn't men be more
desperately dependent on women than they have been
observed to be or claim to be? They need shelter,
biologically speaking. They seek it in women. They
need women, biologically, as much as women need
them!

I could continue debating "the empty vessel theory"
ad infinitum. But I see no value in belaboring what is
most assuredly not a constructive concept. If you believe that you are in a biological trap, then there
would be no point in trying to change yourself and
escape the trap—because your anatomy is one thing
that you cannot change!

As I tell any patient who feels that she is somehow
"doomed" by fate or her physical "ground plan" to be
eternally in orbit around men—"What about mind

over matter? You are, indeed, doomed if you think you're doomed. Wouldn't it be interesting to test fate, or what you regard as fate, to see if, by chance, you might not be as condemned as you've convinced yourself that you are?"

Furthermore, there is much evidence that this so-called female condition of needing men so badly is, in fact, an acquired rather than predestined state. My own experiences with hundreds of patients have convinced me that desperate dependence is learned rather than inborn, culturally induced rather than anatomically based. Because, first of all, I have seen quite a few women become undependent—which would not be the case if desperate dependence were truly woman's biologically based destiny.

And, secondly, when my patients start thinking about the possible origins of their overly dependent behavior, they end up describing not something that was always there but an orientation that developed gradually in the process of growing up female, not just in America but anywhere in the world!

When a woman comes to me and indicates, although not necessarily in so many words, that she feels as if she is nothing without a man, my first objective is to get her to think about what, in her background, could have caused her to feel this way.

I not only urge her to recollect her formative years; I ask her to *record* these memories, to write down all the reasons that she thinks convinced her that the only way to be happy and fulfilled is to become half of a couple. I ask that the list include ways in which her parents might have influenced her to feel this way, as well as cultural cues (ways in which the world-at-large told her who she was supposed to be and how she was supposed to act).

As a result of years of reading these "homework assignments" and discussing them with my patients it is clear to me that one of the most significant reasons for the formation of overly dependent thought and behavior patterns is what I call "The Noah's Ark Factor."

Even as tiny children, we perceive the world as populated by couples, pairs of people, individuals who live and socialize "two-by-two." We are all subject, of course, to the influence of our mothers and fathers as separate entities—but, in addition, and perhaps more importantly in terms of how emotionally dependent we turn out, is the image of mom-and-dad-as-a-couple, our parents as a single unit.

One of my new patients, Marsha, a thirty-two-year-old high school teacher who has never been married, recently described "The Noah's Ark Factor" eloquently:

"I was an incredibly independent child," Marsha told me. "My mother has always marveled at how independent I was. I spent whole weekends reading by myself, entertaining myself. On the whole, I think I was much more self-sufficient at age four than I am now."

"So what do you think happened?" I asked Marsha.

"Well," she said, "when I started really thinking about what could have led me to believe that I'm seriously deficient without a man, I realized that I can't blame either my mother or my father. Neither of them put pressure on me to marry. Actually, it was just the opposite. I was encouraged to excel in school, to be very competitive, to be something great when I grew up.

"So I think that the main reason—the only reason I can think of—that I feel so anxious to be married, or at least shacked up, is merely the fact that my parents were—and are—a great couple. They have a fabulous marriage. They were always inseparable. I never thought of either of them as complete people unto themselves, really. They were My Parents, This Entity, A Couple.

"And it seemed natural and right and wonderful that they should be this way. It seemed like something to which I should—no, something to which I *had to*— aspire. I'm sure that very early in my life I knew, somewhere deep inside, that I could never be happy unless I was part of a winning team like my parents— and that if I failed at this, I'd really be a loser!"

Marsha has a hard act to follow! I've counseled many women who, like Marsha, idealize and want to emulate the glory that was, or is, their parents' marriage—often to the point that they cannot conceive of any other route to deep fulfillment.

On the other hand, many other patients of mine who did not have a model parent-entity like Marsha's, nevertheless came to the same conclusion: that being half of a couple is the only acceptable way to be.

Patricia, a theatrical set designer, lived with her mother after her parents' divorce. "My father split when I was two years old," Patricia explained. "And I remember friends of my mother's, and relatives, clucking sadly over the 'tragedy' of my older brother and me being deprived of a live-in father. Everyone was always fixing my mother up with men, urging her to get hitched.

"Actually, mom didn't need much urging. We had a series of live-in fathers. I noticed when I was very young that when there was no boyfriend in my mother's life, or when things weren't working out with a boyfriend, she'd be irritable, even nasty. Finally, when she married my stepfather, it was like she won the lottery. She landed him! Everyone acted as if she had achieved the *most* marvelous thing a woman could ever achieve."

Susan, another of my patients, spent her earliest years in an orphanage. She was farmed out to foster parents, usually couples. But there was one single-woman foster parent whom she adored. The adoption counselors, however, found that particular woman unacceptable as a parent for little Susan—probably *because* she was single.

Susan was adopted by a couple—a very lovely couple, fortunately. But she never forgot that single woman and the impression she received that there was "something wrong" with this woman, that this woman was defective merely because she lived alone. Susan certainly got the message that "It is better, it is more 'normal,' to go through life paired up with a member of the opposite sex than to live by yourself."

Mary Beth got this message, too, despite the fact that she grew up in what she recalls as "a war zone."

"When I think about my childhood," she told me, "it's like an amorphous din of slamming doors, shouting voices, my mother crying. I don't think two days went by when there wasn't some kind of big battle. You would think that I would have decided that marriage meant misery and avoided it at all costs."

But this was not the case. Mary Beth left college to get married. Three years and two children later, the marriage ended in divorce. Within a year, Mary Beth remarried. She expects this marriage to last, but she told me that "in the unlikely event that it doesn't, I know I'll get married again, or feel I must in order to be happy. I seem to have this compulsion to succeed where my parents failed, to achieve for myself the harmonious monogamy that I know is possible and that I know my parents suffered for not having had."

I have heard some women who came from fractured homes like Mary Beth's espouse, as a result, an entirely different point of view, vowing to avoid marriage, actually fearing marriage as a result of their parents' example.

But the majority of my patients whose parents were unhappily married still grow up believing that couple-hood-is-bliss—because parents are never the only couple-role-models in a child's existence.

Whatever message about marriage you get at home is reinforced or refuted by couples with whom you do not live. Patients frequently mention, in their lists of "How I Got This Way," that all their parents' friends were couples.

So, even if the parents' relationship was less than idyllic, there was a whole little universe of male-female inseparable entities to find and emulate.

Francine, twenty-four years old and just out of law school, told me, "My parents' marriage was a nightmare—although they waited till I went off to school to get divorced. But their friends always came in pairs—to dinner, to parties, to church functions—so I still got the idea that paired was the best way to be.

"And I guess that since all the couples I knew, with the exception of my parents, seemed very much in love and very happy, I just decided that my parents were some kind of aberration. I literally looked up to Auntie Louise and Uncle Jake or Myra and Jim or Sally and Roy.

"Looking back, it's funny but the names of each couple were as inseparable as the people seemed to be. You didn't name them individually—not often. It was always Sally-and-Roy, etc. Like one word."

Francine's view that becoming half of a couple was adulthood's top priority was undoubtedly enhanced by the fact that she did not grow up in the same house with those wonderful couples she admired. She knows, in retrospect, that some of the couples had marriages that were even rockier than her parents'. But because she witnessed, as a child, only couples out in public on their best behavior, she concluded that they, unlike her parents whose problems were all too evident to her, were perfectly mated and perfectly content.

"I was horrified," Francine told me, "when Sally and Roy, by far the most romantic of my parents' friends, got divorced two years ago. I was already in law school. I hadn't seen them for some time. But my childhood impression of their union as indissoluble lived on. When friends of mine, my own age, get divorced I am never shocked. But Sally and Roy? This ideal couple from my parents' circle of ideal couples? Their getting divorced was stupefying! Inconceivable!"

In discussing her childhood, Francine, like other patients of mine, brought up the fact that you see your parents interacting as part of their community.

"The social institutions to which my parents belonged tended to be comprised of couples," Francine said. "I got the idea that you had to be married to belong to the church, to the country club—to belong, period, to anything!"

But the apex of "belonging," according to Francine and many other women I've counseled, was that a man and a woman in a couple belong to each other. A patient recently told me that years after her father died, her mother still insists on being addressed as "Mrs. Louis Simpson." The last name alone wasn't enough; she had to use his first name, too! (This anecdote brought back the stirring final scene of one of the great tearjerkers of all time—the Judy Garland/James Mason version of A Star Is Born—in which Garland, "the star," upon making her first public appearance after the suicide of her alcoholic [and desperately dependent!] husband, referred to herself not by her own famous name but, proudly, as "Mrs. Norman Main.")

Another phenomenon that helped convince my patients that wives have more fun than unattached women were annual holidays, the most exciting times of the year for children.

Holidays come in two major categories—family celebrations and occasions on which couplehood itself is a cause of celebration. The first category includes Christmas, Chanukah, Easter, Passover, and national holidays such as the Fourth of July.

A patient named Janet, who has been married for three years, summed up the dynamics of family-oriented holidays, explaining how these events helped shape her personal history. (She got married several days after graduating from high school and, although the marriage is "hellish," as she says, she is "sticking it out because any marriage is better than being alone.")

"There was a whole lot going on when the family gathered for holidays besides joyous revelry around the groaning board," Janet told me. "First of all, Aunt Edith, the only woman over the age of forty who had never been married in our family's entire history, always stood out, more than ever on holidays, as some kind of pariah. The rest of the family pitied her more with every passing year—and that was pretty obvious to me as a child.

"Then, too, holidays were always so fabulous compared to other days—and it was clear to me at an early age that part of that sense of well-being I felt was because we were a family, solid, normal, a group of related couples and their offspring.

"I reveled in that sense of belonging. I knew that someday, in order to go on belonging, I'd have to have my own mate and my own offspring—that, in fact, with this mate I'd be able to initiate my own family, my own dynasty, my own bountiful holiday celebrations."

Holidays that honor couplehood are even more loaded with implications that love and marriage are more fulfilling than anything else a woman might achieve. Some of my patients have described the fuss their parents made on their anniversaries, commemorating each successive year of togetherness. And their grandparents' anniversary parties were even fancier. "I remember my grandparents' fiftieth," one patient told me. "Fifty years together! It seemed a formidable, earth-shaking accomplishment. I was fifteen then. I remember thinking, 'I hope I'm that lucky or tenacious or whatever it takes.'"

Society underlines the rewards of marriage by placing material value on anniversaries. The greater the number of years, the more costly the symbol. You are more richly rewarded, by implication, with each succeeding lustrum. Wood gives way to silver, silver to gold—then, for all I know, to platinum, uranium . . .

One of my patients mentioned Valentine's Day as having been very exciting to her: "My father always got my mother romantic little gifts—a fancy nightgown, expensive perfume, a ruby ring in the shape of a heart—all the things, come to think of it, that she'd never have bought herself. And I suppose I assumed, from observing this annual custom, that a man is essential to have around because he rewards you for just existing and, through his rewards, you feel wonderful, worthwhile, etc."

No wonder this woman, and so many others, have trouble rewarding themselves! No wonder it never occurs to them that they can do so!

The rewards of love and marriage become obvious to children on ordinary days of the year, too, just by observing their parents' life-style as opposed to their own.

It would be hard to calculate the impact on a child of merely noticing that mom and dad sleep together in the same bed—"and *I* only have my teddy bear. . . ."

One of my friends has a three-year-old son who recently asked her, "When I grow up, will I get to sleep with you like Daddy does?"

"The Noah's Ark Factor," the perception that the whole world is populated by couples and that you, too, have to be part of a couple in order to belong, affects little boys as well as little girls.

The difference—the reason that girls, for the most part, develop more of a life-or-death focus on the opposite sex than boys do—comes with the perception of who does what in the context of couples the child gets to observe.

Beyond the fact of couplehood, we are molded by the behavior of each partner toward the other, the roles each partner plays.

According to my patients, the overriding impression received in childhood of how men and women interact in couplehood was that the woman orients herself around the man—and the man seems much more independent, stronger, self-reliant than the woman.

I get this reading, incidentally, not only from women of my own generation and others who grew up pre-feminism, but from very young women whose mothers reached maturity right along with the women's movement.

My teenage patients identify with my own childhood recollections just as women my age do. I remember my mother being rather helpless in the presence of my father. When I was a child, for example, a bat got into our house. And I remember my mother screaming at me and my sister to put towels over our heads so that the bat wouldn't get tangled in our hair. Then she screamed for my father, who was outside, to come and get rid of the bat. He chased the terrified creature while we, equally terrified, shivered and shook. Our hero vanquished the bat. And my mother was so grateful. And my sister and I, following our mother's example, fell all over him, too, gushing our praise and admiration.

Helplessness has always been regarded, and still is regarded, as an admirable and even glamorous female attribute. Think of the Victorian fainting couches. Camille. Shakespeare's line: "Frailty, thy name is woman." Generation after generation of swooning, clinging, pining heroines of film and fiction illustrated to us that women are an endangered species—women without men, that is.

And both men and women have capitalized on and exploited this image.

Desperately dependent behavior is not always and entirely the result of true feelings of helplessness. My mother, for instance, may well have vanquished the bat by herself had my father or another man not been present. But she learned at an early age, and I learned from her, and even my youngest female patients learned from their adult female role models, to play to a male audience very differently than to a female audience or to themselves alone, themselves-as-audience.

I had one patient who was so knowledgeable about cars that she could have been a professional mechanic. Yet when she was stranded on the highway with a flat tire recently, she stood next to the car, looking as helpless as she could, until help arrived in the form of a chivalrous male motorist—just what she was waiting for, naturally!

And plenty of women scream at the sight of bugs, snakes, mice, or blood—provided they have a male audience to rush to their rescue. Often, however, these same women, when alone, upon encountering a spider, will cold-bloodedly murder it without hesitation.

So female children get the double-edged message that:

1. Acquiring a male partner is the most important life goal.

2. Acting dependent is enormously helpful in both acquiring this male partner and in keeping him around.

In addition to learning to be actually dependent on a man's presence for our very well-being and our acceptance by society, we learn to *act* dependent on males in a variety of ways—and we all have our own ways—in order to attract men and guarantee their continuing presence in our lives.

And this dependent act—playing down our own capabilities, intelligence, courage, etc., while playing up his strength, brilliance, and indispensability—feeds the actual dependence. The act enhances the reality.

So, in a way, we eventually end up brainwashing ourselves!

At a surprisingly early age, your own social life begins to develop along the lines of those of your parents and your parents' friends.

I heard a woman talking recently about her little girl who is three years old. The child's "boyfriend" was coming over after nursery school. "She's madly in love," the mother giggled. "Isn't that adorable? They're a regular little mini-couple."

A patient of mine recalled: "When I was in first grade, my school had a carnival. They had games, clowns, cotton candy—and each class put on a show. My class did a grand ballroom scene and all the little girls wore 'formals' and the boys were dressed up like tiny princes. We were paired off by the teacher. And we waltzed. And the grown-ups loved it!

"I remember being asked, 'Are you going to marry little Tommy when you grow up?' So this image was firmly fixed in my mind: I was definitely going to go through life waltzing on the arm of some man—or some boy, at that point!"

In adolescence it seems (from the point of view of the adolescent) as if all girls fit into one of two categories: those who attract boys and those who don't.

At this point, the importance of male companionship is drummed in through what amounts to tribal rites and customs:

1. You can't go to the prom alone. Or, for that matter, to any formal party. (Informal parties are another story—but you're better off with a date there, too.)

2. Dancing by yourself or with another girl is okay nowadays; discos made dancing a noncontact sport. But the prevailing point of view at dances or at discos is still as it was in my day: It is better to be dancing with a man. Young women today have the same terror of being a wallflower as I did forty years ago.

3. A male by your side in a movie theater, at sports events, even having a hamburger at McDonald's, makes you feel more important—more *visible*, even—than appearing at any of these places alone or with a group of girls.

4. Your self-worth rises according to how many boys ask you out. The more popular you are, the more respect you get from your peers and, hence, the more you respect yourself.

5. *Who* asks you out also affects your feelings of self-worth. If it is the captain of the football team, your self-esteem knows no bounds. If it is the class creep—well, any invitation is better than no invitation, but . . .

Increasingly, by adolescence, parental influence pales by comparison to peer pressure. One patient of mine, who was overweight and unpopular as a teenager, says, "My mother never fussed over me to lose weight so I'd be prettier and get asked out. She never indicated that being popular with boys was all that important. But she didn't have to—I saw for myself how important it was to all the other girls. And I wanted to be like them.

"I saw that the girls who were with guys all the time had more fun. I equated being with boys with having fun. And, dammit, I wanted to have fun—so my goal in life was to lose weight, get pretty, and get popular with the boys, the world's only source of fun, as I saw it."

Occasionally, in my practice, I have counseled women who think they were "lucky" for not having been popular as teenagers. "This made me develop my brains, my sense of humor," one of them told me. "I became my own life-support system because I concluded I could never look to a man for support."

But these women are exceptions. It is by no means guaranteed that the girl who has to entertain herself on Saturday nights will spend that time studying or otherwise working at developing her own interests, being self-sufficient, independent, and strong. Often, the unpopular girl turns out to be just as desperately dependent as her in-demand peer.

She, too, falls prey not only to peer pressure but to what I call the cultural conspiracy—the movies, television shows, popular songs, commercials depicting love as "all you need" (as the Beatles once sang) and lack of love as the worst thing that can happen to you short of death or dismemberment.

Even in movies about something other than love— a spy movie, a murder mystery—the man-and-a-woman theme often wends its way into the plot, as if a love interest automatically makes any story more interesting. No adventure, it seems, is considered more compelling than the romantic adventure—and reiterating this in film and fiction reinforces it as a valid fact of real life.

The all-importance of romance is hammered home, too, in the popular songs that we listen to and dance to, particularly the music we grew up to—and it doesn't matter when you grew up. The message hasn't changed. Swing, rock, soul, country and western, folk, folk-rock, punk-rock—the love songs vastly outnumber the ones about politics, money, patriotism, and world peace.

The music itself may move us, but it is the lyrics with which we identify and through which we confirm and even form our outlook at various times of our lives.

"Every relationship I've had," a single-woman patient commented recently, "has had its soundtrack. There are, in each case, the songs we courted to, the songs we made love to, the songs we broke up to—all these songs reflected our feelings, or my mood, at each stage of the game.

"And always the lyrics say basically the same thing, that love is paramount in anyone's life. And losing love, or not finding it in the first place, is the greatest tragedy in the world."

In my youth, I remember identifying with "Three Little Words" (namely, "I love you") and "All of Me" ("Why not take all of me? . . ."").

For you, the beat may have changed but the subject matter was the same: "My World Is Empty Without

You, Babe," "You're My Everything," "(You're the) Best Thing That Ever Happened to Me," "Stand By Your Man," "It Takes Two."

And girls growing up today are listening to the same, age-old refrain. "Two years ago," a twenty-year-old patient told me, "there was this disco hit, 'Victim,' and the words were about this woman whose boyfriend dumped her. And he had always been unfaithful to her, anyway. And she just hates being a victim, but she knows she'll be back in the same boat, anyway, because every time she turns around she's back in love again.

"I identified like crazy with this song, playing it over and over. It was kind of the story of my life. And at the time, I had just broken up with this guy who was fooling around, just like in the song, and I was determined never to be the victim of a man again. That's what I thought. But at the same time, I was looking for another man, you know?"

Another patient, Deborah, a married woman in her thirties, tells me she was at once infuriated and comforted by a currently popular tune in which the female singer trills joyfully about her man working from nine to five each day and then he comes home to find her waiting for him—as if this were her crowning achievement in life, as if she has achieved nirvana through being a lady-in-waiting.

"The singer really could be me," Deborah explained. "I mean, that's my situation. My life really does revolve around my husband. But I know that's nothing to brag about or set to music!

"I found that hearing this story sung to a bouncy beat was infuriating, because kids listen to these songs, and that message is not one that I would like my daughter to pick up on. But at the same time, I was reassured by the song—because maybe it means I'm not as much of a throwback as I think—or, at least, it means that there are lots of other throwbacks out there who listen to the radio and buy records. I guess the frightening thing is, they might not be as aware as I am that they can make up for all the time they lost living through a man."

There are also movies and television sitcoms about women who are forging their own life-styles. *Private Benjamin* was one of my favorite recent films. And neither Mary Tyler Moore nor her offshoot, Rhoda, seemed to desperately need men in their lives. Billie, the woman reporter on *Lou Grant*, lives alone and seems fine!

But, on the whole, the cultural brainwashing has changed only superficially since I was a young girl. Even little girls who are being brought up "liberated" today, whose mothers encourage them to play with toy hot rods instead of dolls and instill in them the feminist work ethic, are still being programmed, by influences beyond their mothers' control, to be in love with love, to look to love for fulfillment, just as I was.

The other day I saw a commercial on daytime television for "Starr," one of those dolls that comes with accessories, including a toy telephone. The doll was dressed in a cheerleader costume. And two little girls were gurgling delightedly over her. One girl said, "Starr's popular!" And the other one piped up, "And she's a cheerleader!" I couldn't believe I was seeing this in 1981!

Nor could I believe a current perfume commercial in which a disembodied male voice asks the beautiful model, "Why do you wear this perfume?"

"Because it smells good," says the model.

"Confess!" commands the voice.

"Because *he* likes it!"

There are more subtle commercials, too, the ones that pass off liberated behavior as if it meant true liberation—for instance, the Harvey's Bristol Cream pitch in which we see the woman-as-predator, luring the man into her lair—but it's "downright upright" because of the particular drink she's serving—Harvey's Bristol Cream.

In this little scenario, we see that a woman can do what men have always traditionally done—take the initiative, call him up, invite him over. But the modern woman who calls the shots may well be just the same old dependent female using a new technique and language to assure herself of male companionship.

She is not demonstrating emotional maturity, undependence. She's still exemplifying men-are-my-top-priority behavior—but with a new color icing on the same old cake.

At this point in therapy most women have begun to feel that they are up against a formidable challenge. It seems impossible to break ways of thinking and behaving that are so deeply rooted, established in early childhood, reinforced by cultural definitions of who you are supposed to be and how you are *supposed to* act.

And I usually meet with arguments when I point out that what they have come to view as the only right way to live—as half of a couple—is not, in fact, the only right way.

You are not, for instance, either a woman with a male partner who is content (as long as he's there) or a woman without a man who is therefore miserable. You are not limited to two alternatives—one invariably good and the other invariably bad.

"Okay, I believe you!" a patient recently shouted at me. "Maybe I can be happy alone. Maybe I shouldn't look to men for real fulfillment. Maybe I can find it within myself. But you know something? I don't want to adjust to being single. I like men. I want one in my life. I want you to tell me what I can do to have one in my life. . . ."

I told this woman that, since she wanted to remain convinced that monogamy is the only road to bliss, I would let her in on a secret. Her attitude, her anxiousness—and I didn't say "desperation," just her anxiousness to find someone—is undoubtedly picked up by every man she meets. She may not tell the men she dates what she told me—but they probably sense it, anyway.

I advised her that if she really does want a man, what she has to change is her attitude. She has to rid herself of that anxiety, whatever it consists of—that time is running out or that she doesn't want to grow old alone, or just discomfort at not having a permanent, live-in date for whatever her contemporary versions of The Prom are.

She has to reach the point where it truly doesn't matter if she has a man or not. She'll enjoy life anyway.

I assured her that she would see—as I've seen with other patients—that the minute a woman decides to live her life to the fullest, to make her life more interesting and exciting, the minute she stops waiting for a man to jazz up her days and nights, that is when Prince Charming is likely to come down the pike!

But I can't give guarantees. And I always make it clear that if you say to yourself, "Okay, now I'm going to start *acting* totally autonomous. I'll show men I don't need them!" then the strategy I just outlined is not going to work.

The idea is to get beyond even worrying about the fact that your apartment is currently no-man's-land, to operate at full speed because you pivot around your own inner core of security and are convinced, deep down, that you'll be productive and happy whether or not you ever find Prince Charming.

If you have this attitude, you win either way.

And you are now well on your way to this self-constructive, new outlook—although you may not feel as if you are.

Awareness is always the first step toward change, a bigger step than you might think. And you are already aware of what desperate dependence means *to you*, and what, in your background, caused you to believe that a man is so vital to your well-being.

Now the idea is to use this awareness to become undependent.

Thinking that you are nothing without a man, to whatever extent, is a major assumption that you have made about your life as a result of having grown up in a society that places so much importance on The Couple.

But this major assumption is comprised of smaller assumptions that you make daily, in any number of situations. These smaller assumptions are based on the way you think you and other people are *supposed to* think and feel and act, according to your experiences, according to your upbringing.

For instance, Sharon, my patient who remembered her father giving her mother "romantic little gifts" on Valentine's Day, was horribly disappointed and angry when her new boyfriend ignored her birthday. "I reminded him seventeen times," Sharon said. "Then the great day came and—nothing."

So Sharon assumed, as a result of the way she thought men who cared about women are *supposed to* act, that this man didn't care about her. She took her disappointment out on her boyfriend, sulking, being sarcastic, doing anything but openly admitting what was bothering her. So she ended up ruining her own birthday.

I pointed this out to Sharon, adding that, instead of making the automatic assumption that the man ignored her birthday and therefore didn't care, why not challenge this (and other, similarly based) assumptions. Why not consider the possibility that there might be other reasons, having nothing to do with you or his feelings for you, why he failed to get a birthday gift. For instance:

1. He might have been so preoccupied with his own problems that he simply forgot your birthday—even after seventeen reminders.

2. Maybe he was short of cash and too embarrassed to admit it. He figures he'll get a belated gift when he has enough money to buy something terrific.

3. Maybe he has no idea what you like and is going to ask your advice.

4. Maybe birthdays weren't a big deal in his family—in other words, presents weren't a tradition. Not everyone was brought up just like you, you know!

Had Sharon stopped to realistically analyze the situation at hand, instead of jumping to a self-deprecating conclusion based on her own supposed-to's, she might have waited for her boyfriend's explanation. Or, had no explanation been forthcoming, she might have asked for one in a non-accusing, undemanding way. She wouldn't have felt put down; she wouldn't have alienated her boyfriend with what seemed to him to be unjustified bitchy behavior. She might, in short, have had a happy birthday, gift or no gift.

And what does all this have to do with getting over thinking you are nothing without a man?

Well, a woman who pivots around her own inner core of security, rather than waiting for a man to make her feel wanted, loved, worthwhile, etc., wouldn't need that birthday gift. She might want it; she might appreciate it. But she wouldn't *need* it. Her self-esteem wouldn't rise or fall as a result of receiving it or not receiving it. So the latter eventuality would not make her suffer—and lead her to "punish" him. She would not, in other words, fall into a desperately dependent behavior pattern.

And a woman who does *not* pivot around her own inner core of security can start to develop that second backbone by learning, in a situation like this and in many other situations, to realistically assess what is going on rather than reacting according to her supposed-to's.

Desperately needing a token of affection (and not for nothing are they called "tokens" of affection) from a man to affirm self-worth is but one example of the sort of supposed-to thinking that, multiplied many times and applied to many aspects of your life in the course of your average day and week, adds up to the major assumption we're trying to get rid of: thinking that you are nothing without a man.

It is by challenging each such *supposed to* that you will chip away at desperate dependence until it is gone. Although, as I said, I do not espouse formulas for self-improvement, I have observed that overly dependent behavior, like other negative habits, can be obliterated through challenging the assumptions that comprise it, the assumptions that come from the way you've been conditioned to think and act.

I have also observed that this examination of a situation from all sides in order to understand it, and in order to behave according to reality and not according to supposed-to thinking, is not easy at first.

Radically changing your thinking and behaving habits, like altering bad eating habits, or any bad habits, is seldom comfortable at the beginning. Thinking for yourself at all times takes effort.

But once you become committed to the idea that you are going to challenge your supposed-to thinking and replace it with a more realistic approach, the process becomes an exciting adventure. Once you get beyond your own resistance, change becomes far more compelling than remaining at a psychological standstill.

And as you challenge each *supposed to* in each situation, you become more skilled as a challenger and more aware of yourself. And your new ways of thinking and behaving become as automatic as the old ones were.

I often liken this process to practicing a piece on the piano. You play it clumsily at first, then more smoothly. Then, if you keep working at it, there comes a point at which you own it. It's in your fingers. Playing it becomes a flow. You no longer think about each and every note.

And that is what happens after a certain period of self-conscious striving to challenge all the supposed-to's in your life. Eventually—and I can't tell you at exactly what point you will go on automatic pilot—you will discover that you have become undependent. You will feel that you have developed a strong second backbone—and you will derive your security and sense of well-being from that, rather than searching for it in the presence of a man or in a man's behavior toward you.

You might want a man, and appreciate him. But you won't desperately need him. As a result, you'll be happier. And any relationship you have will be better.

So let's get to work, starting with the area that is more loaded with supposed-to's than anything else: sex.

III
Becoming Sexually Undependent

I think that I have heard every conceivable reason for desperately needing a man. But the main one, according to my patients, is "sex."

The thing is, they don't always mean sex. They mean all the real or imagined side benefits of sex. A patient named Lisa put it this way: "What I need is the feeling of security that I get from sex, the feeling of being desirable that a man gives me by wanting to go to bed with me. If a man is attracted to me sexually, then I feel worthwhile."

Many women are convinced that having a man make love to them makes them beautiful, sexy, desirable, etc. It's like the *Good Housekeeping* Seal of Approval.

I've heard hundreds of supposed-to's that dominate women's sexual behavior and, consequently, their relationships with men. But all of these supposed-to's fall into four basic categories:

1. If you are living with a man: The quantity and quality of sexual encounters per day, week,

or month is a yardstick by which you can measure his love for you (hence, the success of the relationship). If a man loves you, he is *supposed to* demonstrate this physically—ardently and often!

2. If you are not living with a man: Sexual involvement implies emotional commitment. If you sleep with a man he is *supposed to* ask you out again.

3. Men are *supposed to* place great good looks above all other qualities a woman might possess in seeking out a mate. Therefore, you require a man's attention to make you confident about your appearance.

4. Sex is *supposed to* be right up there with a healthy diet in maintaining your mental and physical health. Therefore, having a man around is as important as having food in the refrigerator.

Now let's examine each of these supposed-to's, and their consequences, the ways in which they lead to overly dependent behavior, more closely.

My friend Barbara has always operated according to Supposed-To #1. She truly believes that the caliber of her sex life indicates the success of her marriage.

Barbara is a studio photographer whose specialty is taking still lifes of everything from jewelry to baby food for print advertisements. Her career is flourishing. To her clients, Barbara seems competent, confident—perhaps even tough. In her relationship with Hal, her husband of five years, Barbara does not manifest the symptoms of desperate dependence that I described in Chapter I—not for the most part, anyway.

But where sex is concerned, Barbara was, as she put it, "a basket case." Barbara insisted that Hal make love with her every night—because, if he didn't, that meant (she assumed) he no longer loved her as much as she loved him.

Barbara put enormous pressure on Hal to perform sexually, to fulfill the quota of commitment-confirmation she considered mandatory.

Ironically, Barbara did not have an unusually active libido. She craved sex as an affirmation of the depth and permanence of her relationship.

Let's look into the behavior that resulted from Barbara's *supposed to* attitude. Let's say it's 11:30 on a Tuesday evening. Barbara and Hal are in bed. The news is over, and Barbara reaches for the remote control device to turn off the television, snuggling up to Hal as she does so. "Don't turn off the TV," Hal says. "I want to watch *Nightline*."

"I want to turn it off—and turn you on," Barbara murmurs.

But Hal would rather watch television. Barbara lies there, her eyes on the television screen and her mind elsewhere, busily mulling over various automatic assumptions about Hal's behavior:

1. He no longer finds me sexy.

2. He doesn't love me as much as he used to.

3. He might be having an affair—or thinking about it!

62 °

Panicked, Barbara continues to make physical overtures to Hal, preventing him from concentrating on the television show, let alone enjoying the program. Finally, Hal gets up and goes into another room to watch television.

Barbara is devastated! Hal, in one swift motion, has confirmed all her worst suspicions. She gets up, follows Hal into the other room, and accuses him in a loud voice of not loving her anymore.

When Barbara described this situation to me, I told her that she was not only causing herself undue misery; she was putting undue strain on Hal, possibly causing the demise of the relationship—in other words, *she* (not Hal) was contributing to her nightmare coming true. Eventually, if Barbara kept up the demanding, accusing, clinging behavior, Hal would leave the house, not just the bedroom.

I suggested that Barbara stop expecting Hal's behavior to conform to the way she has always thought men are supposed to behave. I urged her to challenge the assumptions she makes because of her *supposed to* expectations—and to start dealing with reality rather than acting on those assumptions.

Focusing on the particular Tuesday night situation that I just described, Barbara could have thought of many possible interpretations for Hal's behavior that would not make Hal the villain and her the victim:

1. Maybe Hal did, in fact, want to see *Nightline* because the subject was of interest to him.

2. Hal may have felt ill.

3. Hal might have been preoccupied with a job-related problem; it's difficult to perform in bed when your mind's in the office.

4. Hal just plain might not have felt like making love. Men are *not* always ready, willing, and able.

Barbara, like many women I know, made the mistake of taking too personally what she read as Hal's rejection, so anxious was she for his sexual endorsement to validate his love for her and the permanence of the union.

Barbara's reaction to Hal's desire for television, rather than sex, had she taken it at face value, might have been to ask herself, first of all, whether she really did want sex at that moment and then to figure out why she wanted sex, what she hoped to get out of it. There are several possibilities, and since Hal was unwilling, for whatever reason, to cooperate, there are several things that Barbara, herself, could have done:

1. I want sheer physical relief—an orgasm. (In that case, there is no reason why I can't do it myself.)

2. I want to stop feeling so empty. (In that case, sex is far from the only fulfilling pursuit in the world, or even in the house. There's the spy thriller I'm in the middle of reading. I can work on my dissertation. I can even concentrate on *Nightline*. I might learn something.)

3. I want to get relaxed enough to fall asleep quickly. (In that case, I can do yoga or cal-

isthenics or have a glass of white wine or a cup of hot milk.)

4. I need emotional support. I want to feel wanted. (In that case, I can call my best friend and pour my heart out to her. Or, after *Nightline* is over, maybe Hal and I can just have a good talk.)

One factor that makes challenging sexual supposed-to's difficult in the beginning is that so many women have never defined themselves sexually or in terms of their interaction with the opposite sex. Barbara, for instance, found it difficult to figure out what she wanted from sex at any given time because she never had a clear idea of what sex meant to her or what her sexual needs were—except for the vague notion that sex is supposed to be equated with a man loving her and declaring his intention to keep on loving her. And except for her related assumption that unless a man is performing this function for you, you cannot be a whole, fulfilled, fully functioning human being.

I find that lack of sexual definition is a common problem not just among married women like Barbara, but for single women, too—particularly for those who subscribe to #2 Supposed-To: that sex should lead to emotional commitment—or, at least, to another date.

Roberta was a patient of mine who espoused this point of view. When she entered therapy, she was thirty-three years old, fed up with dating, and actively looking for someone who embodied her rather stringent qualifications for Ideal Husband. Roberta desperately wanted to get married, or at least to have a man fall in love with her. Therefore, she was desperately anxious to please and impress any man she regarded as potential true love and modern romance material.

I presented Roberta with a hypothetical situation that I often bring up with female patients:

Let's say that you are about to go out on your second date with a man. Let's say that this is a guy whom you really like. You relish the thought of being with him. You revel in just looking at his distinguished profile as he drives the car. You get all dressed up for the great date. You're feeling gala. You think you look terrific. You think, "This could be the start of something big!"

Now—what would you like to have happen on this date? Putting aside what you think he would like to have happen—what do *you* want?

Roberta pondered for several minutes, started to say something, then stopped, and finally blurted out: "Nothing. I don't know what I want. I mean, I want whatever he wants."

I have had patients who have responded differently: for instance, "I want to rush with him to the nearest motel and consummate my infatuation." But that is not the usual answer. The usual answer resembles Roberta's. "I don't know what I want." Or "I want *him* to like me." Or "I want him to want to make love with me."

And I say, "Stop it! Forget what *he* wants and tell me what *you* want." And they sweat for the "right" answer, for what they're supposed to want, and come up with—"Nothing."

They have no idea that their bodies are entitled to want something. This just never occurs to them. They rely on the man to make every move, because:

1. "If I please him, he'll come back."
2. "Even if this doesn't turn out to be 'forever,' I do need him to come back because otherwise I'll feel like nothing . . ."

Now, what happens when a woman behaves on a date according to all this *supposed to* thinking?

Pamela, a teacher who is as eager to hook a husband as Roberta, told me that one assumption she always makes when embarking on a date with "someone possible" is that the man's top priority for the evening is sex.

"So I think," Pamela explained, "that if I go along with his program, he could decide that I'm 'an easy lay' and not even consider having a serious relationship with me. On the other hand, if I say, 'no,' he might conclude I'm too prudish and not want to see me anymore."

I've heard many variations on Pamela's worries. They all have in common the preoccupation with what he wants, rather than what you want, and the assumption that he wants sex, accompanied by assumptions about how he will react if you do or do not cooperate.

I point out to patients such as Pamela that the solution to this dating conundrum is as simple as knowing what you want and acting accordingly. I asked her, "What if you allowed yourself to admit when going on a first date with a man you really like that, in addition to the planned activity (the ballet, the movie, the meal), you would like something to happen sexually. What, exactly, would you like to have happen? Or—what among sexual activities would please you the most?"

"To be hugged and kissed," Pamela said, promptly.

"Have you ever considered that that might be exactly what the man would like—and no more?"

"No."

Okay, it is true that some men do embark on a date with very little but sex on their minds. It is even true that some men are total cads, and if a woman is not interested in sex, they are not interested in her.

In this case—and usually you know, in your heart of hearts, if this is the case—you should feel relieved, not rejected, when you don't hear from the cad again.

But discounting cads, and discounting the insecure fellow whose eagerness to "score" comes from his own fear of sexual dysfunction, let's look into male prerogatives a little more carefully.

First of all, men have always been under an enormous amount of pressure because of the burden of responsibility women place on them. The men I have interviewed, patients and friends, are nearly all aware that many women do not know what they want on a date, sexually or otherwise.

"Everything is left up to me," Marty, a thirty-one-year-old lawyer, complained. "Everything from the logistics of the date to the future of the relationship. Women look to me to make even less than earthshaking decisions such as which movie to see, what restaurant to go to, should we walk or take the car.

"I'll say to a woman, 'Well, where do you want to have dinner?' And she doesn't know whether she wants Italian, Chinese, Greek, Mexican, or steak. She says she'll be happy with wherever I decide to go. She just wants me to be happy. It's infuriating!"

Hence, the single man's burden. It was brought up recently in *The New York Times* in an article entitled "In Dating, Men Remain the More Troubled Sex." Reporter Marilyn Machlowitz pointed out that "Despite the widespread belief that dating practices are changing rapidly in the United States, psychologists report that traditional patterns remain. The anxiety associated with dating is still preponderantly the problem of men, and men still initiate dates in the vast majority of instances. . . . men still face more pressure to initiate dates and thereby run the risk of rejection when they do. . . ."

I wouldn't say that my male patients have more problems with dating than my female patients. But they are certainly as troubled as women. Most importantly, men's concerns tend to be strikingly similar to those of women, and so do their attitudes and expectations. Often enough, they, too, are confused about what they want sexually.

What I tell those female patients who are always acting according to what they think men want and expect are some hard truths about what men really do want and expect—according to what they have told me:

1. Men may act independent and aggressive because society demands it of them (even as passivity is an acceptable female trait). But they are often just as insecure and, therefore, as vulnerable, as women.

□ 69

2. Men fear rejection, too.

3. A man is generally eager to please a woman he likes for the same reason (initially) that she wants to please him—to avoid rejection, to get another date and, perhaps, an actual relationship with her.

4. Sexual intercourse is not always foremost on a man's mind on the first, second, or third date—or even on later dates. Men who are in touch with how they feel and who they are (as opposed to the I'm-A-Man image they concoct in response to what they perceive as society's and women's expectations) frequently tell me that they get a great deal of enjoyment out of "just necking," as my patient Marty put it.

"Women tend to exaggerate a man's lust quotient," Marty explained, "his need for genital-to-genital contact. But it all depends on the situation, my mood, who the woman is. Often, hugging or touching or hand holding is just fine, just what I want. I mean, if I like a woman a lot, I can wait. I'm not some sex-crazed adolescent, after all."

I find that informing women about men's real feelings (and, incidentally, vice versa) is a very useful therapeutic tool in dealing with desperate dependence. In order to get a patient to stop acting on assumptions and start viewing situations realistically, she—or he—has to understand how much men and women have in common emotionally.

I have come to believe that the single most important factor in becoming undependent in relationships with the opposite sex is playing down the word "opposite" and all the obstacles to understanding that go with it.

The social rituals that have been going on for ages—men and women both acting out their supposed-to's—throw up giant barriers to understanding how alike men and women really are. Unfortunately, many fictional and film treatments of Love Today, as well as well-meant, advice-filled articles and books, suggest rather superficial solutions to what ails men and women in love or looking for love. The solutions tend to revolve around women learning to be more assertive, more independent, more like men traditionally are *supposed to* be, and men learning to be more expressive of their feelings, gentler, more like women traditionally are *supposed to* be.

But the solution to dating (and mating) problems is not role-reversal. It is role dropping. If men and women would interact as plain people, there would be less "Him Tarzan, Me Jane" thinking and no need for "Him Jane, Me Tarzan." Women wouldn't cling; men wouldn't encourage their clinging. Desperate dependence, on both sides, would give way to more humanistic (rather than male-female) ways of interacting.

Because of the problems and fears and insecurities that men and women share, it stands to reason that a woman who gets to understand herself better will also come to understand men more. In learning to treat herself more kindly, she will also end up being more compassionate toward men. In ceasing to see herself as victim in so many instances, she will stop viewing him as villain.

When a woman comes to me, as my patient Jeanne recently did, in tears because she went out with a man, slept with him—and now, two weeks later, he still hasn't called her back, I try to get her to think about him and his behavior in terms of herself—not in terms of what she assumes that all men are like.

The He-Didn't-Call-Me-Back situation is one that I encounter so frequently in my practice that it has become, to me, a metaphor for male-female relations. I use it frequently as a showcase for getting people to regard dating as *human* relations. Once they can do that, the crucial phone call becomes less crucial. The patient stops looking to the date's approval/endorsement for self-validation. The patient thereby strengthens her own inner core of security, becoming more undependent, more emotionally self-reliant.

Jeanne, twenty-three years old, has been living alone in Manhattan for six months—"on my own," as she said, "for the first time in my life. My parents always took care of me; then college replaced my home environment. Now I'm out there, looking for some man to take care of me, I guess."

Jeanne works as an editorial assistant at a prestigious women's magazine. She met Larry, a young advertising executive, at a party given by a mutual friend. "He seemed like a great guy," she told me. "Witty, bright, with the kind of looks that improve with age." (Jeanne, you notice, was already planning for a possible future with Larry three seconds after meeting him!)

Larry asked Jeanne to go out to dinner with him at his favorite Szechuan restaurant. (Jeanne hates Chinese food; however, she pretended, for the sake of her possible future with Larry, that she was addicted to it!)

"After dinner," Jeanne told me, "we walked for a long time, ending up back at my place. And then, you know, your stereotypical scene took place. I offered him coffee. He let me know he wanted more than coffee. And I went along with him because, well, I really liked him, and I wanted to see him again. But I guess he didn't feel about me the way I felt about him, because I haven't heard from him since."

Jeanne regarded Larry's silence as a tragedy. She wondered what she had done wrong. She wondered if she were a sexual zero. She wondered how, since she had made it so obvious to him how much she liked him, he could be so callous as to not call her. In short, she concluded that since this one man, Larry, had rejected her, she must be rejectable in every way—not pretty enough, not amusing enough, not sexy enough.

I asked Jeanne if she had ever gone out with a man who was good-looking, witty, successful—but just not her type. And when he asked her to go out again, she turned him down—because, although she knew he liked her a lot and she recognized his good qualities, she just didn't want to pursue the relationship?

"Sure," Jeanne said.

"Well, what if that was how Larry felt about you? What if he thought you were attractive, bright—but not 'his type' for some reason? If you allow yourself the privilege of not seeing a man again, for whatever reason, why can't you allow a man the privilege of choosing not to go out with you again? Furthermore, why, if he does not call back, do you think it's an indictment of your self-worth? When you've turned down dates with men, it didn't mean *they* were ugly, stupid, or that no other woman would ever be interested in them, did it?"

"I never thought about it that way," Jeanne said.

In order to encourage Jeanne to view situations like this objectively, to give her more perspectives, based on reality and not on automatic assumptions, I read her a list of other possible reasons that Larry might not have called—reasons culled from an article by novelist David Bradley in *Savvy* magazine.

The article was entitled "A Man Explains: Why I Said 'I'll Call You' and Didn't." I found Bradley's point of view particularly valid because he based all his explanations for men not calling women on ways that women have acted toward men and should, therefore, understand:

1. "A man might decide that a wonderful night or weekend should not be spoiled by trying to make it more."

2. ". . . a man, especially if he is both sensitive and realistic, might have doubts about how he feels, about how she feels, and therefore sit paralyzed before his phone."

3. ". . . a man who is not sure what he wants or what she wants may never take up the phone to explore the possibilities."

4. ". . . a man might put off calling until he gets one or two little things cleared up . . . until it's just too late."

74 °

So, as Jeanne began to understand, it is a mistake to allow so much of your self-esteem to rest on whether or not a man calls back. It is a mistake to look to him, to wait for his phone call (which you equate with his approval) for your own feelings of self-worth. Understanding that his silence is not a condemnation of you as a person enables you to rely on your own, developing inner core of security rather than relying on him or on other men to make you feel secure.

Furthermore, it is a fact that reliance on your own inner core of security enhances the possibility that a man will call back. There is another reason for a man not asking a woman out again that David Bradley mentions in his article: "a man (might choose) to let an affair he has found in some way lacking die in merciful silence."

Now, this would seem to confirm Jeanne's—and other women's—fears. "Lacking! I'm in some way lacking!"

But the woman is not usually lacking in the ways that she thinks (such as, not pretty enough, not sexy, tall, blonde, short, etc., enough).

According to men with whom I have discussed this business of a woman "lacking" something, the problem is actually her behavior as a result of fearing she will in some way fail to enchant him, to please him, to get him to come back. In other words, her very reliance on his approval, her very failure to have firmly established that all-important core of security within herself, is what makes her "lacking."

What I frequently do, when a woman tells me she feels severely rejected by a man, is to ask her to have this man call and set up an appointment to see me. Such sessions generally take place at the patient's expense, since I use this information as a resource. They are confidential, unless I'm given permission to discuss them with my patient (which happens more often than not). His side of the story is often that he felt, somehow, that the woman "wasn't there." Or, as Larry put it when I called him and asked why he hadn't asked Jeanne out again: "She wasn't really with it. She wasn't participating in the date. I didn't detect any real interest in me. I mean, I know she liked me—but I got the idea that maybe it was an act because she really wasn't paying attention to what I was saying. Even when we made love, I felt like she was a million miles away."

So Larry, who was initially very interested in Jeanne, lost his interest. Jeanne, like many women desperate to "hook" a man, lost out because her anxiety over "hooking" Larry was all too apparent to him in the form of her being "a million miles away."

What she was doing, in her head, giving her that abstracted air, was mulling over all her supposed-to's and how she should act and be as a result of them: "I wish I had worn more makeup." Or "I'm too fat." Or "I wish I could have thought of a brilliant thing to say to keep the conversation going."

Had Jeanne been secure in herself, and not expected Larry to make her feel secure, she might, in fact, have gotten what she wanted. The phone call. Another date. Maybe a relationship.

But Jeanne, unfortunately, was operating according to Supposed-To #3: Being good-looking is *supposed to* be of paramount importance in getting and keeping a man. Therefore, his sexual interest is the only way I can have that "Movie Star" feeling of being beautiful, desirable, glamorous, worthwhile.

Jeanne was so anxious for that "Movie Star" feeling, and so conscious of the flaws that might prevent Larry from giving it to her, that she did, indeed, make herself unattractive to him.

But it wasn't her extra five pounds that turned him off.

And it wasn't the pimple.

And it wasn't her makeup.

It was her attitude that was "lacking."

If you feel good about yourself physically—or, at least, if you manage to stop dwelling on every real or imagined flaw—you will not need a man's sexual interest for your self-validation. And this undependent attitude, ironically, will free you to be more interested in, therefore more interesting to, a man. More attractive, in other words.

Now, in order to gain more confidence about the way you look, to build up this particular aspect of your inner core of security, it is necessary to understand the origins of insecurity about your appearance.

There are many possible reasons that a woman, however beautiful, may feel unattractive. The most common is simple sibling rivalry. You might have had a sister or brother who was considered "the beauty of the family," or was merely younger than you. A baby always gets much more attention than an older child. And the older child often interprets this attention as meaning that the baby is prettier and that everyone likes the baby more. So, from the moment the baby arrives on the scene, some older children begin to feel insecure.

Childhood slights can also cause deep, long-lasting damage to your self-image. People struggle all their lives to stop suffering from schoolyard taunts and nicknames mocking some aspect of their looks.

Furthermore, our culture throws out all sorts of roadblocks preventing us from achieving self-confidence about our appearance. For one thing, every year brings some new Ideal Woman. In recent years, many a patient of mine has felt woefully inadequate compared to Farrah Fawcett. Then Suzanne Somers. Then Bo Derek, the perfect "10," whose preeminence in the media caused patients to actually come to me complaining that they were "only a seven" or "Next to her, I'm a goddamned two!"

I liked Bette Midler's self-assessment during the year of the film, 10. When Barbara Walters asked her what number she thought she was on a scale of one to ten, Midler said, "Fifty-five!" I wish more women would be able to feel this way about themselves.

In addition to having the seemingly flawless movie star and model images—as well as society's general overemphasis on youth and beauty—to contend with, women are encouraged to take a fragmented view of their own looks. And this is really the heart of the problem. Cosmetic ads generally promote one product for one part of the face or body. For example, a certain eye shadow will make your eyes unforgettable. A certain lipstick will make your mouth luscious, particularly if you learn how to put it on properly, thereby correcting your mouth's imperfect shape. By using such-and-such shampoo, your hair will be thicker or shinier or healthier or free of embarrassing white flakes.

It is no wonder that the self-image of many a woman would resemble, if rendered in oils, a Cubist painting.

One day you might feel repulsive because you forgot to shave and have five o'clock shadow from your knees to your ankles. The next day, you have a hive on your face. Although people aren't turning to point at you on the street, you feel as if they are. The hive might as well be engraved in neon. Another day, you might be dwelling on your eyes being too close set, your nose being crooked, your teeth being less than pearllike, your extreme height, your too-ample thighs, two extra pounds on your waistline, a new wrinkle.

So many of my patients are preoccupied with their parts rather than just seeing themselves as total, integrated human beings.

Wouldn't it be better, instead of fretting about real or imagined faults here and there, to adopt the attitude: "I'm me—and the essence of me, my whole self, is what counts."

When Leonardo da Vinci painted the *Mona Lisa*, he captured the essence of that woman's personality. Millions upon millions of people have looked at the Mona Lisa and been struck by her great beauty. They do not stop and say, "Mona Lisa's smile isn't wide enough. Her eyes aren't big enough. That hairstyle isn't flattering to her." We don't look at the painting that way. We respond to the essence of that woman that shines through, something mysterious, something kind, something altogether fascinating.

And, if the truth be known, men do not usually look at you part by part. Men are not usually aware of the flaws in this or that part that drive you to distraction—that make you act so distracted!

Men are not necessarily looking for physical perfection in women. They may well stare at a gorgeous woman—but then you do, too, if only to compare yourself with her and to study what makes her so gorgeous. But I've come to the conclusion that beauty is not the deciding factor for men wanting to spend time, let alone a lifetime, with women. Because I've noticed, often, that a woman who may be far from a "10" may have hordes of men interested in her.

I have a patient right now whom I would certainly not describe as beautiful, or even pretty. She's somewhat overweight and has a bland face. And yet she really does not know what to do with all the attention she gets from men. And the reason is very simple. She enjoys herself. She enjoys other people. Instead of worrying about what everyone thinks of her—and how they view her and that she must remember to exhibit her left profile at all times because it's better than her right—she's busy focusing on other people and throwing her whole self into every relationship and every situation. And that's what comes through. And it is beautiful—far more beautiful than a perfectly symmetrical nose on a worried, fretful, self-involved, insecure woman.

If you feel joyful about yourself, if you enjoy being you, then that quality will show up on your face, in the way you walk, talk, actively engage with other people (not just men). There is nothing more attractive than this quality of liking yourself. And I'm not talking about being conceited or narcissistic. I'm talking about the good synchronization with yourself, which comes through working at getting rid of a fragmented self-image that causes you to be obsessed with getting this or that part of you up to par in order for you to be worthy of some man so he can make you feel attractive.

Only you can give yourself a positive self-image. A man, no matter how turned on he proclaims himself to be, can't do it for you in the long run. Often, when a man expresses sexual desire for a very insecure woman, she concludes that there's something wrong with *him*! Or, should they hit it off, she eventually turns him off with her constant demands for reassurance via sex or verbal assurances of his continuing sexual interest.

It is possible, of course, to experience a burst of self-confidence through a man's sexual interest in you— but basically the security that you're looking for must come from within you if you want to feel loveable on a permanent basis, whether or not you have a lover.

We have now seen the fallacy of operating according to the premise that you need sex (i.e., a man) to feel desirable and, once there is an emotional commitment, safe from the horrors of life alone.

We've also seen that the healthy ego can feed itself without a man's help.

But some patients would comment at this point, subscribing as they do to Supposed-To #4, that "I still need a man for sex—even if there's no romance attached. Sex is necessary for survival. Like food."

But, in fact, sex is not as necessary as food. Many people, men and women, can and do go through long periods, months and even years, without experiencing sex—sometimes of their own free will (because of all-consuming career concerns, for instance) and sometimes for lack of a suitable partner. And the word "suitable" is the key here. You could substitute "worthwhile," "desirable," or the adjective of your choice as long as it's a positive one.

The point is, any man is *not* better than no man. In the film *An Unmarried Woman*, when the woman played by Jill Clayburgh, after having been left by her husband, goes to bed with the lecherous guy who's been pursuing her, just in order to make love—with someone, anyone male—the viewer might well conclude that she probably would have been better off staying home and reading a good book or going to a concert or, for that matter, masturbating.

But all too many women persist in feeling that sex with a man is the greatest form of entertainment, far preferable than anything you might undertake on your own: like reading, going to a concert, or—especially—masturbating.

Although very few women today believe that masturbation can make you blind or give you warts, you'd never guess they were that advanced in their thinking from the blushes and downward glances I get when I mention it to my patients.

These inhibitions about discussing masturbation, let alone doing it, do not usually stem from guilt. Some women are embarrassed because if they do it, they assume this means they're not as successful as they're supposed to be with men; and, they feel, it's silly and futile to masturbate since masturbation is not supposed to be as satisfying as sex with a real, live man.

As one of my patients commented, "I like the orgasms that men give me much better than what I can do myself."

Notice her phraseology: "The orgasms that men *give me.*"

But, in fact, when you are making love with a man, the orgasms that you have occur not only because the man is moving a certain way or touching a certain area (or areas), but because you have turned on the orgasm switch in your head and allowed yourself to climax. It is a physiological fact that if your mind is otherwise occupied, if you're angry or thinking about bills you have to pay, or just not feeling passionate, that man can do every tactile trick he knows, and you will not have an orgasm.

Men are not necessary for you to have a *proper* orgasm. The ones you might have by yourself feel just as good, objectively speaking. You may well prefer sex with a man to sex by yourself—but that is not because he is indispensable. It is because you have brain-washed yourself into thinking that he's indispensable.

Now you can brainwash yourself out of this particular assumption. Because what if you hit a dry run? What if you've only been meeting creeps lately? Or, if you're married, what if your husband is so anxious about his failing business that your sex life is failing, too?

More and more of my patients who are in any of these situations are making a miraculous discovery.

Take Jane, for instance, who, despite occasional fears about ending up like the woman in *Looking for Mr. Goodbar*, continued her life-style of satisfying her sexual "needs" with men she picked up in bars and elsewhere. She once likened sex with these characters to going to the dentist: "Well, I don't really like to do it. But I *have* to do it, you know. Keeps me healthy."

Jane did not define herself as promiscuous. "I'm very discriminating," she said. "I only sleep with men who are real good-looking and have at least a ninth grade education."

While Jane was recuperating from a bad case of the flu, during which time she was too weak for a social life, she did some serious thinking. "I thought about what all my sexual experiences were adding up to—and the answer was nothing, not even instant gratification much of the time. I realized that, for the most part, I'd get more out of watching TV."

For months, Jane did not go out with a man. "I was really celibate—and I discovered that I did not become ill or crazy as a result. My vagina did not rust. Now, when I go out, it's because I want to, not because I assume I need to. I do it out of choice, not desperation. And when I sleep with a man, I get more out of it—because I'm doing it out of real desire, not because I think it's *supposed to* keep me healthy or assuage loneliness or get me approval."

Jane has found other resources for pleasures and sustenance she thought only men could give her. Many of my other patients have done the same thing. We'll look into these alternatives in the following chapters.

IV
Learning
To
Love
Being
Alone

I don't want to be alone!" so many of my patients tell me, by way of explaining why a relationship with a man is so crucial to their well-being.

But, as I am quick to point out to these patients, having a man who loves you is no guarantee that you'll never be alone. Even if the man lives with you, you'll still spend time alone. That, I *can* guarantee!

Some of the loneliest people I know are married. Yet my single patients tend to regard marriage as the best cure for loneliness. And my married patients tend to be terrified of becoming un-married because that, to them, looks like a vista of unmitigated, unbroken loneliness.

I've had many a married woman confide, "I hope *I* die before he does." This is by no means a noble, unselfish sentiment. It does not mean "Gee, life is so wonderful. I truly hope he gets to have more of it than I do!" What it really means is "Better he should suffer the tortures of loneliness than me!"

I have come to take a dim view of romantic accolades, such as "If something happens to you, darling—God forbid—I couldn't go on living." To me, such statements are made not so much out of love for the other person but out of lack of love for yourself.

You might as well say "Since I can't stand living by myself, it's nice having you around to amuse me from time to time." Only, of course, that doesn't sound nearly as romantic, as flattering, as overstating the case and making the guy feel that, next to your heart and other vital organs, he's the only thing that keeps you going.

The thing is, although many a woman thinks that just having a man come along and take a starring role in her life will prevent her from ever having the problem of loneliness again, this assumption really isn't true.

Loneliness is something that everyone has to face.

Single women must face the fact that a man is not going to prevent it.

Women who live with men must face the fact that these men cannot devote all their time and energy to keeping them from feeling empty.

And women who live with men must also face the fact, should the relationship end because of his death or departure, or for any other reason, that they must be able to survive alone—and that they can, in fact, thrive without a man.

Now, before we examine this supposedly terrible thing—being alone—in the hope of proving that it really is only as terrible as you make it, let's investigate this widespread assumption that men have magical powers that protect women from loneliness.

Claire, who is thirty-two and has been married for seven years, was a firm subscriber to this belief when she came to me for therapy. Claire is a social worker and her husband, Max, is a doctor. Although Claire enjoys her job and the opportunities it gives her to help other people, she enjoys the time she spends with Max even more.

After several sessions with Claire, it became apparent to me that she is, first, Max's wife and, secondly, a professional woman with a degree in social work. She spends every evening with Max in front of the television set or "out," with mutual friends, couples who form their "circle."

As for weekends, I asked Claire if she ever has lunch or goes shopping with a female friend on a Saturday, and she assured me that she never does anything on Saturdays and Sundays without Max. "I get so little time with him as it is," she said. "He often works later than I do. Weekends are our real time together. I'd never do anything to cut into that."

I asked Claire if she had ever gone out of town without Max—say, for a convention of other professionals in her field—and she replied that she had not only never done so, she'd never even considered such a thing.

You may be wondering why, with a relationship so idyllic that Claire couldn't conceive of even taking an afternoon off from it—why would she seek the help of a therapist? Well, Claire was unhappy. She didn't know why she was unhappy. She couldn't define her unhappiness, either. She just suffered from those vague, empty feelings, a nagging fear that sometimes was mysterious in origin and, at other times, was clearly anticipation of some future shock: "What if something happens to Max?" Or "What if Max falls out of love with me?"

I asked Claire what her interests were—other than her work. It turned out that she played bridge, went sailing on the small boat Max had recently bought, and had recently taken up photography.

But—and here is the vital point—Claire did not like playing bridge or sailing or photography. Those, in fact, were Max's major hobbies. Max was passionate about all three pursuits. He encouraged Claire to take them up—and she didn't need much encouragement because, to her way of thinking, showing an interest in your husband's interests is essential to marriage maintenance.

Claire's philosophy is today's version of the old cheerleader technique. Once upon a time, wives thought that showing enormous fascination with their husbands' hobbies and pastimes—not to mention their careers—would make their husbands happy and, therefore, keep their husbands devoted. Nowadays, many women adopt their husbands' hobbies as their own rather than merely standing on the side, cheerleading.

Claire's life boils down to fulfilling her supposed-to's and fighting her fears:

1. The good wife is *supposed to* have a great deal in common with her husband and share all his interests.

2. If she doesn't, there are many other women around who will, and he might, one day, fall in love with one of them. And then—

3. "I will lose him. I will be alone."

And, of course, Claire's outlook derives from her deeply rooted assumption that a husband is *supposed to* provide your life with meaning and, concomitantly, keep you from ever being listless and bored.

It took a while to convince Claire that this point of view was somewhat babyish, to put it bluntly. "According to your way of thinking," I told her, "you are *supposed to* go through life—with Max making sure there's never a dull moment, finding hobbies for you, helping you become proficient in these hobbies. It's as if you're a little girl with Max perpetually chucking you under the chin, dangling pacifiers in your face, cooing to you, and cajoling you to learn to read!"

Finally, Claire started realizing that if she were unhappy, it wasn't Max's fault, any more than it was Max's obligation to make her happy. She admitted to herself, and then to Max, that there were lots of other things she'd rather do with her spare time than play bridge, sail, and take pictures.

Claire, after careful thought, decided that she truly loved to paint. She wanted to perfect her knowledge of French and go on to study other languages. She had always loved tennis but gave it up because Max found it boring.

Now all this might sound like a sugarcoated pill sort of solution—but merely pursuing a hobby that your mate does not care for is not, in itself, the solution that I am suggesting.

The answer is in your attitude. Instead of the if-he's-pleased-then-I'm-pleased attitude, I'm suggesting a please-yourself attitude. Not "please yourself and damn the torpedoes," however.

You and your husband can have things in common. For instance, both Claire and Max love to garden. They've always done this together; there's no reason that they shouldn't go on doing this. In fact, I highly recommend it.

But, from now on, instead of going along with Max's program in every respect, Claire feels free to express herself through her own pursuits. Every once in a while, she'll join the bridge game just to be sociable or if Max and the other players are hard up for a fourth. Or she'll go sailing. But no more slavishly shadowing Max from bridge to sailing to photo expeditions (or, for that matter, exhibitions).

Claire no longer assumes, you see, that truly being herself—to the point that she has to spend periods of time away from Max, even at times when Max isn't working—will erode their relationship. She recognizes that her little "vacations" away from their relationship—Saturday afternoon shopping with friends, for instance—will not propel Max into the arms of another woman.

She realizes, above all, that if the predominant emotion you feel every day is fear, that if you are preoccupied with "what if's"—the big one being "What if he leaves me?"—then you're not fulfilling your potential as an individual, and, in fact, you're crippling the potential of the relationship.

It's the psychological equivalent of bound feet, this panic at the thought of losing him. You are unable to reach into the depths of yourself and allow everything that's unique inside you to flower. Instead, you expend your time, energy, and imagination on being an appendage of someone else.

But fear of losing him is not the only reason that women abdicate so much of themselves in a relationship. There's something else, something more subtle, happening. There is another fear—"What if I delve into myself and discover that none of my interests are compatible with his, that I shouldn't be living with him, that the only reason I am living with him is fear of being alone and that, despite the huge investment we have together in property and children I would probably be happier without him?"

I've counseled several women who were afraid to admit what they knew, to face evidence of what they suspected—so they went on blindly applying first aid to the relationship, existing rather than living, pursuing a life that they felt, deep inside, was not really theirs—or not what they wanted. Because the alternative—being alone even for whatever amount of time it took for them to find some new man—appeared so frightening.

Joan, thirty-eight, had been married to Howard for fifteen years when she came to me for therapy. But they had known each other for at least twenty-five years. They dated on and off during high school, then more steadily when they were in college. "I've had very little experience—I mean, serious involve-ments—with other men," Joan said. "I'd go out on dates and I guess I had a few one-nighters when Howard and I were mad at each other, but I never really had a relationship with anyone else."

When Joan came to me for therapy, she complained of being constantly depressed. "And I have no reason to be depressed," she said. She described her elegant life-style—Howard was an extremely successful corpo-rate lawyer—the ultramodern suburban home that had been featured in an Italian design magazine, the summer home on Martha's Vineyard, the Maserati.

"You know where I get to drive the Maserati?" Joan asked. "To the supermarket. To the shopping center. Sometimes I daydream about driving in the Indianap-olis 500. Or I imagine myself as a Hollywood stunt-woman. What if I had been a stuntwoman? Or I see myself as a photojournalist, covering El Salvador. I envy those reporters on TV. I envy Lois Lane, for God's sake! Isn't that ridiculous?"

Given Joan's background, it wasn't at all ridiculous. She had majored in journalism in college and had worked for a year for a wire service before getting married. Since her marriage, however, her reportorial career had consisted of occasional freelance jobs for her local paper—"covering such scintillating events as Junior League luncheons, shopping center promo-tions—I can't seem to get away from these shopping centers."

Until last year, when Joan's daughter turned thir-teen, much of Joan's time was devoted to mothering. "But now Julie has her own life; she's very much the liberated little woman, studying hard, busy with all kinds of clubs. Her average day makes me dizzy."

As for Howard, "Well, we love each other—but we've grown apart. Our conversations are mostly logistical—'Shall we get new screens for the sunporch?' That sort of thing. I wouldn't tell him my crazy dreams because he'd agree with me instantly. They're crazy. I guess the biggest thing we don't have in common anymore is that he's content with his life. I'm not. I want more. I could have had much more."

After several sessions, Joan admitted that Howard had actually become a stranger to her, that she no longer felt at home in her home; that she longed to actively pursue at least one "crazy" dream, to take up her journalism career again. She had brought this up with Howard, and he had told her, "I don't want a working wife." Joan, in short, admitted that she wanted a divorce—and that was the first time that she had admitted this to herself.

But she had all sorts of excuses for staying married:

1. Getting divorced would be terribly hard on her daughter.
2. Joan's parents, who loved Howard, would probably never speak to her again.
3. Divorcing Howard would be an act of sheer ingratitude—look at all he had done for her.
4. What if I don't make it as a journalist? (And Joan did not want to be a "charity case," living on alimony.)

But all of these excuses masked Joan's real reason for her reluctance to face life on her own: She felt that a woman alone was someone to be pitied. A woman without a Mrs. in front of her name was inevitably some kind of social outcast. She equated being alone with being lonely. She didn't "know how" to be alone.

I asked Joan if she had ever considered how much time she spends alone as a married woman. Her daughter, Julie, had her own life. Howard worked overtime.

"Yes," Joan said, "but I always know they're coming home. So I never feel really, ultimately alone. But I do get lonely even now. There are huge chunks of time when I have nothing to do, and that's when I daydream. Sometimes I go off to the movies. I try to escape from my life—from myself, actually."

Joan's problem was much more complicated than the situations of the women who have come to me wanting to end short-term dead-end relationships with men and not being able to do so because they also fear the alternative—which they perceive as unmitigated loneliness.

Joan had a lot to lose: the comfortable life-style she had helped to create, a group of friends who saw her as Howard's wife, an identity, a sense of belonging that she was used to and that meant much more to her self-image than all the material goods Howard provided.

But helping Joan resolve what she regarded as her no-win situation involved the same lines of discussion that crop up in my dealings with women whose relationships are clearly destructive to them. One of the most extreme examples of clinging to a miserable marital situation (out of the conviction that being with any man is better than being alone) was Tracy, whose alcoholic husband frequently beat her.

Tracy, who was twenty-four when she began therapy, kept telling me that she couldn't leave her husband because he "needed" her; she alone could help him. "It isn't *him* being brutal," she insisted. "It's the booze. When he's sober, he's as gentle as a lamb."

Again, this attitude was an excuse, a cover-up for Tracy's real feelings:

1. I really don't love him anymore, but—
2. I can't make it alone.

Both Joan and Tracy had to become aware that, however much they thought they'd lose by striking out on their own, they'd lose more if they didn't. They had to learn to stop regarding the "alone state" as some big empty vacuum out there in which they'd be free-floating. One of the tricks of coping with aloneness is to fill that vast imagined space with plans, activities, and goals.

To bring this concept down to a more practical level, I asked both Joan and Tracy to make lists, each night, of how they'd fill the next day. Eventually, each of these women accustomed herself to a structured schedule instead of waking up to an amorphous series of hours in which she struggled to overcome her depression, having nothing better to do.

Both stories have happy endings. Both women got divorced with relatively little trauma. Joan moved back to her hometown, Chicago, and works for a newspaper. Her daughter, Julie, spends summers with her. Julie chose to remain with her father during the school year so that she wouldn't have to leave the environment, and friends, she loved. Joan feels that the satisfaction she's earned from her new life "and being my own woman" has enhanced her relationship with her daughter. "Julie respects me more. We have much more in common. We're as much friends as we are mother/daughter."

Tracy also moved back to her hometown—Los Angeles. She chose to get her own apartment, rather than live with her parents. She is working toward a master's degree in business administration, supporting herself with a secretarial job—"Sometimes I long for a few *empty* hours here and there!" she told me over the phone.

Interestingly, Tracy's husband, with whom she keeps in touch, was sufficiently jolted by her departure that he sought treatment for his alcoholism. "But I'd never go back to him," Tracy says. "He wasn't right for me to start out with. And, in the end, he really was just a buffer against loneliness."

Neither Joan nor Tracy had easy, snag-free adjustments to living alone. Joan once likened it to stopping smoking. "At first, I really missed my comfortable old role of Mrs., which had become like a bad habit because it kept me from being me! And then sometimes I felt almost manic—I was so happy to be free of the Mrs. But you level off; you get acclimated.

"I do have moments, particularly when I see a seemingly happy couple on the street or in a restaurant or something, of sorely missing being married. But they pass."

I can tell you, and other women who have been there can tell you, that being alone can be wonderful, that it is certainly far preferable to a stultifying relationship, that by ending a relationship that is a dead end for any reason and embracing life alone, you will be freer to develop fully as an individual. So taking what you may view as a huge risk can be worth it.

But the value of aloneness is something that you have to discover for yourself. Truly enjoying yourself, actually having a good relationship with yourself, which is the prerequisite to being able to get the most out of living either alone or with someone else, is not something that you can make yourself do overnight or simply by following some therapeutic rite, mine or someone else's.

Some people are blessed with an inborn capacity to enjoy themselves by themselves. I have a close friend, Angela, who is in her fifties and has never been married. She has had several long-term relationships with men and nearly got married once. "But," she says, "it would have meant giving up too much."

Angela owns her own house in San Francisco. Every square inch of her charming Victorian-style home reflects her tastes and the places she has traveled. Angela travels extensively in her career as a political organizer and lecturer.

"But even in San Francisco, I'm making new discoveries all the time, learning, as if I were constantly dropping in on different cultures and countries. I have been politically involved since college. Now my work takes me to all of the wide variety of neighborhoods in this marvelous city. I'm always plunging into different little worlds, meeting people of all backgrounds, people with concerns I may never have thought of but come to share as I work with them, virtually living among them."

Angela has told me she rarely feels bored or lonely—"although everyone, inevitably, must experience those feelings sometimes. And then you just kind of muddle through."

There was a period, however, when Angela found it difficult to "muddle through."

"I had just suffered the end of a very important relationship with a man—we lived together for two years. He was younger. But there were many other reasons that it wasn't going to work out. Rather than prolong the agony by growing even more attached to him, I decided to end it. And then, around the same time, my mother, with whom I was very close, died suddenly.

"I had been seeing a psychoanalyst and had stopped seeing him shortly before all this happened. So I went back to him. I told him, 'I feel, all the time, as if I were alone on top of a mountain and there is no way to come down.' He said, 'What about Ted?' (Angela's boyfriend.) I told him that was over. Then he said, 'What about your mother?' I told him she had died.

"He said, 'You *are* alone on top of a mountain!' In other words, I was justified in my feelings of isolation, emptiness, aloneness. I was reacting normally to a very real situation. We are all, ultimately, alone—and that wouldn't be such a cliché if it weren't so true.

"Just *knowing* that you are not alone in your ultimate aloneness, that you have this in common with every other human being, is helpful, in itself, in alleviating those empty feelings.

"But what has really been my salvation since my mother died, since Ted's departure, has been my extended family, which is how I think of this community. It was a renewed commitment to community involvement—not a new boyfriend—that saved me. There is so much to be done in this city. So many people need me. I have found that my dependence on all the people in those different neighborhoods and their dependence on me is as sustaining as any relationship I've ever had with a man.

"You're only as alone as you want to be. There's a whole world out there—next door, down the block, across town or across the ocean for that matter! Is Mother Teresa lonely? I doubt it! Not that I'm recommending everyone to go out and save the world. But just saving a little bit of it may also save you!

"As for coping with just plain being by myself in my house and avoiding wallowing in loneliness—one thing I rely on is my 'memory bank.' I've had a rich and fairly exciting life. I surround myself with mementos from every stage of it, every stopping-off point. I find myself, thinking about where I've been and people I've known, reliving those experiences, seeing them in new lights. It's fascinating—and a real weapon against loneliness.

"How can I feel empty, I ask myself, when my life has always been and still is, so full?"

Many women Angela's age—and younger—regard age itself as a threat. "Being alone when you're young isn't so terrible," one of my patients told me recently.

"But when you're older? When your chances of ever marrying are slimmer? When you lose your looks and therefore your ability to attract men? I'm having a great time now, dating three different men. But I'm thirty-four. Time is running out!"

Angela's attitude toward aging is far more constructive. She feels, and I agree with her, that it is far better to view getting older according to what you gain with the years rather than what you lose. "I am more able to relish being alone now than I was years ago," Angela says. "I've become far more secure as I've grown older. And the more secure you are, the less aloneness scares you."

Just as the process of living can contribute to insecurity (because you become more aware of how fragile human beings are, of economic realities, of your own limitations, etc.), life's experiences can also nourish your inner resources. You become more and more equipped to deal with frightening or threatening situations. And, as situations in life go, aloneness is far from the most frightening!

Merely getting a certain amount of living under your belt does help you feel more anchored. As you get to know yourself better, you trust yourself more. You do stop being afraid to be with yourself, alone.

Not that every older person is a bastion of self-confidence and healthy egocentricity—far from it! Life equips you to deal with living only if you let it.

If you don't let it, if you're stuck in this notion that you need a man to pull you through this thing called life, then, of course, you're not going to allow life to teach you anything, and you're not going to learn to live it better.

You do have to *learn* to live well. And learning about aloneness is part of nearly everyone's life experience. Although I don't have all the answers for everyone, I have learned some things from my own life that you can think about and probably use.

When I recall those occasions when I have been unmarried and alone, one of the things that I did was to see a therapist. And, as I've discovered in my role as a therapist, I was far from the only person who viewed a therapist in that light—as a paid companion, a person to whom I could go at a certain hour every week and pay that person and have that person listen to me. So that one hour a week, I could count on the therapist to assuage my loneliness.

As I tell my patients who are counting on me to counteract their loneliness for one hour a week, this may well be a good temporary measure, but it is far from a loneliness cure. Nor is it a valid use of therapy on a permanent basis.

I'm making two points here. One is that if I, as a practicing therapist, sought out a colleague and paid her, in essence, to keep me company, then I certainly understand how anyone could have a rough time being alone. And I sympathize. And I'd never claim that aloneness is easy to love.

The second point is that constantly avoiding aloneness, never permitting yourself to face that empty house or apartment (whether through visiting a therapist or compulsive dating or ongoing partying or staying at the office until one A.M.) is no way to learn to love being alone.

You may not even have to learn to love being alone. If you can stand the hyperactivity it takes to never face it, that's fine. Most people can't.

So let's face it—aloneness, that is. What exactly is it that scares people so much about living alone?

I've found, in my practice, that the answer for many people is "dying alone." Or "having nobody to take care of me should I become incapacitated"—as if having a mate on the premises, someone who loves you, could ward off accidents, disease—even death. Or make all of the above easier to take.

Our "supposed-to's" even include death and dying! I get the impression that many of my female patients think that there is a "right" way to die—and that the "ideal" death was exquisitely portrayed by Ali McGraw in *Love Story*.

There she was, pale and lovely and fading fast, with Ryan O'Neal by her side and, ultimately, climbing into bed with her, battling the intravenous tubes, to "hold her." All of which was merely the medical center version of *Camille*.

But, in real life, even if you're married you might well end up dying alone. You can't take him with you! And, in fact, if you do become terribly ill, the person you're going to spend the most time with is the night nurse at the hospital.

So much for male companionship as a balm in the event of your loss of health!

Another leading cause of terror of aloneness is thinking of it as a permanent state (not unlike death).

But aloneness is not so terrifying if you view it as I do, as a one-day-at-a-time situation.

For instance, I went on a vacation recently to the Yucatán. My husband had to work, so I went alone. At my hotel, I met some fascinating people with whom I spent all my time. But one evening I came down for dinner later than usual and found that my little group had decamped without me.

I admit that for several minutes I felt abandoned, then annoyed, then unpopular. ("So! They all secretly didn't like me!") Had I continued thinking in that vein, I would have quickly gone on to being panicked at the very idea of having an entire evening to fill without anyone else's help—i.e., an empty evening. And that's what the evening would have become—empty, time wasted fretting about my lack of companionship.

As it was, I went downtown to a restaurant that I hadn't yet tried. I happen to adore Mexican cuisine, and I was fascinated by the differences between the dishes of the Yucatán and elsewhere in Mexico. So at dinner, I discovered several local dishes. Some were great; one, I choked on! I didn't take a book with me to the restaurant to divert me from my aloneness. Instead, I tried following the suggestion of M. F. K. Fisher, who writes elegantly not only about food but about the atmosphere in which you can best appreciate it—that is, I concentrated totally on what I was eating, what was in the various dishes, making each bite an adventure.

Between courses, I studied (as subtly as possible) the other people in the restaurant, guessing where they were from, what were their relationships to one another, even making up little histories and character sketches for them. (People-watching is one of the best loneliness and boredom cures there is—it can even make an event out of standing in line at the bank!)

After dinner, I took a walk and browsed in some shops that were still open. Then I went back to my room, where I had some good reading material that I hadn't even begun to tackle—and this was my opportunity to make some headway with my overly ambitious reading plans for that trip. So I did.

And the next day was, as Scarlett O'Hara said, another day. My newfound friends, it turned out, thought *I* had gone off without them. I shared my experiences of the night before with them—and vice versa—which, in a way, was more interesting than had we all shared one experience together.

So the popular truism "nothing is forever" is not only a fashionably cynical way to view relationships. It applies also to aloneness—and to loneliness.

But what if fate decrees that you will be alone, not forever but for a long time, long enough so that you'd have to endure bouts of loneliness? What is loneliness, anyway? Many people think the word is synonymous with boredom—and, although that's not a literal definition, that is what loneliness consists of for quite a few of us.

A friend of mine changed her attitude toward aloneness remarkably—and became far more enthusiastic about life in general—when she made the simple discovery that she did not have to do what she thought was appropriate, what she was supposed to do, what had become rote behavior, in one particular situation.

She had always become depressed when watching a sunset alone and not with some man's arms around her. She always felt there was something vacuous and wrong about seeing a sunset—or, for that matter, a dramatic thunderstorm, a sunrise, waves lapping up on the beach—without a lover there to validate and enhance the experience.

But one evening, she became fascinated with the colors of the setting sun and, for some reason, focused only on what she was experiencing and how she felt—and not on who wasn't there seeing it with her.

She let herself thrill to the experience, become involved with the experience. And it was a revelation.

The longing for a lover to validate your experience of a natural phenomenon, or to validate any experience, is related to window-sitting—it is yet another way in which women act out the way they think they ought to be. (And the origins of this particular supposed-to are not difficult to trace. Think of all the movies we've seen in which a sunset rarely appeared without two heads, male and female, silhouetted against it!)

But there is no way you ought to be or have to be.

One of my patients, a poet, once observed, during a solitary trip to Greece, that "to see the Parthenon, you really have to have four eyes." (Needless to say, she felt the same way about sunsets.)

But when I went to the Parthenon, I was so glad my husband was back in America. His pace is different from mine; he would have slowed me down, reading each inscription, making me impatient. As it was, I thoroughly enjoyed myself.

To recap, two effective ways to take the boredom out of aloneness are:

1. Concentrating on the experience rather than on who could have been sharing it with you and isn't.

2. Being aware of (although not dwelling on) the advantages of experiencing something alone. Often enough, the presence of another person, however much you love him, can detract, not enhance, an event.

But there are more reasons that you might be unable to get deeply absorbed in *the moment*, wherever it is:

1. Sometimes, the "I" interferes with the experience. For example, it is difficult to lose yourself in the beauties of a natural or man-made wonder when you are actually wondering: "Do I look okay?" "Was that handsome man over there looking at me—or her?" "Why didn't I wear my black slacks? Here I am looking drab in the middle of the Piazza di Spagna, crossroads of some of the world's sexiest men!"

2. Sometimes, you're so preoccupied with your problems that the outside world can't make a dent. Navel staring can nullify even the most fascinating experience. There you are, face to

face with the Sphinx, and all you can think is: "God, why does my ankle ache? Maybe it's arthritis!" Or: "Why didn't I bring my Valium? I feel so anxious." No wonder you're bored! All you're experiencing is your own inner broken record of laments. You might as well have stayed home.

3. Another cause of boredom is actually canceling out the present because you're so busy plotting about what is going to be. For instance, after spending two minutes admiring the sunset: "Well, the sunset sure is beautiful! Better get back inside. Jack might've called and left a message on the machine, and I really want to see him tonight."

I call this attitude "future block." The future—your plans for it—totally block out your absorption in the present.

Another version of future block is scheming how to *use* the experience, rather than just reveling in it. A writer friend of mine is always so busy taking notes and pictures everywhere she goes that she hardly knows where she is at any given time. "You never know," she says, "when I'll be able to use that material. In my memoirs, in a novel . . ."

For her, just standing still and watching and listening is excruciatingly boring; she doesn't know how to participate in just being; she has to package life.

If she'd stop fretting about how she'll use what she's seeing and just stop and see it, she'd never feel lonely and bored without her notebooks and cameras. And, in the long run, she'd probably be able to write more profoundly because she would feel her experiences more profoundly.

The antidote to boredom—the only one, as far as I know—is true involvement in something to the point that you forget all about yourself, your health, your marital status, your undifferentiated feelings of anxiety and—especially—what's going to happen next, where you're going to go, or what you're going to accomplish.

One of my favorite quotes—and, as it happens, very good advice to all those who get bored when left to their own devices—is from Norman Douglas's novel, *South Wind*: "Delve deeply; (but) not too deeply . . . into yourself. . . . Delve into the living world and strive to bind yourself to its movement by a chain of its own welding. . . . Externalize yourself!"

It is good, also, to keep in mind that you are never really alone when you perceive of *yourself* as a fascinating companion. A friend of mine gave this positive summation of how to love being alone: "Living alone is just like being married—except the relationship you are having is with yourself. Like marriage, living alone has its ups and downs. Sometimes you hate yourself, and sometimes you love yourself. Sometimes you get along with yourself; sometimes, you're at odds with yourself. There are days you find yourself fascinating and days you find yourself to be an unutterable pain in the ass. And here is where my little analogy falls apart. Because one thing you can't do alone, as in marriage, is to stalk into the other room and slam the door in your face!"

It's important, too, to recognize the supposed-to's built into our aversion to aloneness—and to eradicate them.

Some activities, for instance, are *supposed to* be social. So we consider it antisocial—and an invitation to misery—to pursue them alone. Meals are a good example. Being able to get through a meal in a restaurant alone has practically become a symbol of "liberated" singlehood. There have been many magazine articles advising women how to accomplish this feat.

I've already described my solitary meal in the Yucatán. Part of the fascination there, the boredom antidote, was the exoticism. This, of course, is missing when I dine in a New York coffeeshop or in my apartment on evenings when my husband works late or goes out.

On those occasions, I turn what could be a lonely event into a chance to lose a few ounces, at least, by eating cottage cheese and fruit instead of the pot roast I'd serve my husband, who has no figure problems, and be unable to resist myself. So the fact that I am getting some benefit out of dining alone takes the edge off it, making me enjoy it.

Going to bed at night is another lonely time—particularly if you're used to sleeping with a man. But again, you can turn it into an opportunity to accomplish something for yourself. For example, I feel that I am disturbing my husband when I read in bed because the light and the sound of pages turning bothers him. But I love to read in bed. It's a luxury. So when he is out of town, I always go to bed early and read for hours.

There are many other advantages to being alone:

1. You can get up in the middle of the night and play records as loudly as you want (assuming the neighbors don't mind).

2. You can wake up at five A.M. and go for a walk without coming back to your disgruntled mate who is muttering, "Where the hell were you?"

3. You don't have to pick up anyone else's socks (or anything else, for that matter).

4. Your whole apartment or house (not just a room of your own) can reflect you—with your memorabilia, your color schemes, your photos, etc.

5. You can leave tomorrow for Paris without thinking twice or asking permission or seeking approval from anyone.

6. You can walk around with a hideous-looking moisturizing mask on your face at any time without fear of turning anyone off.

7. The bathroom is all yours, all the time.

8. You can go on a three-day fast without being tempted by someone who brings home Tasty-Kake and pizza.

9. You don't have to worry about a mate's worries, only your own.

10. Your apartment or home can be as sloppy as you like—and no one will accuse you of slovenliness.

11. Your apartment or home can be as neat as you like, and nobody will (a) mess it up, or (b) accuse you on a regular basis of being an anal compulsive.

12. You can make two-hour, long-distance phone calls, and nobody will interrupt midway to complain about your extravagance.

13. You can subscribe to a whole season of classical concerts without worrying about offending someone whose idea of great music is Michael Jackson. Conversely, you can indulge your taste in rock concerts every other night, if you want, without worrying about offending someone who refuses to listen to anything more recent than Bach.

14. You can dress entirely according to your own taste—and no one will try to prevent your expressing yourself via a new hairdo, more of a décolletage, throwing out your entire wardrobe and replacing it with jumpsuits in every color, etc.

15. You can sing around the house, and nobody will make disparaging faces or remarks.

16. You can pout and pose and frown and grin at yourself in the mirror—without getting caught and made to feel silly.

17. Your sex life can be as wild or as tame as you wish. You have only yourself to please.

18. You can accept a job offer anywhere in the world and take off without considering anyone's priorities but your own.

19. Your refrigerator need not contain anything you don't like.

20. You can have any pet you wish without considering another person's possible aversion to animals—or his allergies.

21. You can choose your own friends without being constrained by another person's possible dislike of people you like.

Make your own list. Write down every possible way you can think of that you can call your own shots and make your own rules—because you're alone.

But be sure to include that last item—choosing your own friends. .

Your greatest resource in learning to be something without a man is yourself—liking yourself, feeling complete in yourself. But friends, as you're about to discover, do help—probably more than you think.

V
Woman: A Woman's Best Friend

More dependence on—and enjoyment of—other women means less dependence on—and more positive enjoyment of—the special man in your life.

Good, strong female friendships are an invaluable source of emotional support, solace, information, knowledge, entertainment, and just plain companionship.

I remember my college days, when I would sit around giggling and gossiping with my dorm-mates. There was a quality of intimacy, warmth, and delight to those "gab sessions," and also in my friendships at the all-girls' camp where I spent many summers. Throughout my life, too, women have been there in my moments of tragedy, to commiserate with me, care for me, comfort me.

And yet, I've found that many of my female patients do not appreciate the tremendous support system they could have if they took female friendship more seriously. All too many women greatly underestimate the great and sustaining power of sisterhood.

Before getting into the reasons that female friendship is so often given short shrift in our social priorities, and before discussing ways to initiate friendships more successfully and to maintain friendships more effectively, I'd like to discuss in more detail the ways in which female friendships can be rewarding enough to help dissipate dependence on the man in your life, or on the man you wish were in your life.

One of my patients, Margaret, recently gave me a wonderful statement about what her close friendships with women mean to her: "There is just a general understanding that women have among themselves. Being a woman brings with it certain emotional and physical states that women don't have to explain to each other. It's like sharing an emotional and physical context in which some rapport is automatic—not that I could become best friends with every woman— beyond the bond of being female, there is a kind of chemistry, not unlike what happens when you experience mutual attraction with a man. But instead of being sexual, this chemistry consists of outlook, interests, experiences in common.

"But the odd thing is, it's the female bond, not the other things in common, that count most. My best friend is a woman who couldn't be more different from me in looks, style, ambitions, income, background. Yet we have this incredible understanding. She's always there for me and vice versa. She's as important to me as my husband—although I'd never tell him that. But there are levels on which she and I communicate that could never occur between my husband and me."

I asked Margaret, and some of my other patients who have told me that female friendships mean a lot to them, to think about the ways in which their lives have been enriched by their friends. Here are some of the qualities of good female friendship that they mentioned:

1. There are subjects of interest to women that men find "silly" or "boring." I know that the cliché situation of the women going to one side of the room after dinner and discussing diapers and the men going to the other side of the room and discussing world events is anathematic to any woman with even the slightest feminist bent. But the fact remains—many women do like to discuss makeup, clothes, recipes, and the like (as well as weightier subjects, of course). And your woman friends are a far more receptive and responsive audience where these topics are concerned than most men, including the one who loves you.

2. It is often easier to discuss your sexual phobias, fantasies, problems, with women rather than with men. A woman will understand your feelings about sex better than nearly any man, including most male gynecologists, simply because you and she share an anatomical makeup and psychological experiences that men do not share with you.

Two women can communicate about sexual matters in graphic detail without the embarrassment that they might feel in unburdening themselves, *revealing* themselves, to this extent with men.

Also, there is often the fear, in confessing your insecurities or lack of knowledge about sex to a man, that this will turn him off or in some way take the romance out of the relationship. Such barriers exist much less frequently in discussing sex with a woman friend.

And you can learn a lot about sex from other women, both technically and in arriving at certain comforting realizations—for instance: "So other women also wonder if they're frigid!" Or "So I'm not the only woman who's not sure if she ever had a multiple orgasm!"

Several of my patients tell me that they, and their woman friends, have been known to "compare notes" to see if "we're doing certain things right." Conversations like this are consoling and instructive—and far easier to have with women than with men, particularly with *the* man.

3. A woman friend can help you recognize, pinpoint, sort out, and resolve problems with men or with a particular man. Sometimes you can't confront him with your grievances—but you can tell another woman. And she can give you the benefits of her experience—or, at the very least, serve as a sympathetic listener while you talk out your problem and resolve it yourself.

4. There are certain elements that sometimes mar a male-female love relationship but usually don't threaten female friendships—namely strong feelings of ownership or possessiveness that derive from insisting on sexual exclusivity; the need men and women often feel to withhold certain parts of their pasts or feelings from a mate in order to preserve an aura of mystery or simply out of fear that the mate might be disillusioned.

Female friendships tend not to be as volatile as love affairs. They are more easygoing, more relaxed, less threatening in terms of opportunities to hurt and be hurt, and, generally, more open and honest.

5. You can almost always be yourself with a female friend—and, often, behavior with a man is calculated, fabricated, fraught with ulterior motives. (I do not recommend this sort of behavior with men but, according to my observations, that's the way women sometimes do act.)

As one patient put it, "With a woman friend I can say anything that comes to mind. I don't have to worry about how I look. I can look good, bad, indifferent, frumpy, fat, frizzy-haired—and it doesn't matter. You don't feel you have to impress a woman friend with your looks or profundity or wit or anything.

"Really, the bottom line is that being with a close woman friend is like being with yourself."

6. Women who are best friends tend to mother each other—and you do not generally get this type of nurturing from a man. "I don't care what

anyone says about men becoming more emotionally attuned to women's needs," one patient said. "You have to describe 'mothering' to them, give them examples of it, and then keep reminding them. A good woman friend just knows how to be maternal and when to be nurturing and when to stop."

Margaret succinctly summed up the female friend phenomenon: "The only thing a man can be to you that a woman can't be is your lover— assuming that you're heterosexual!"

And many of my patients ended their observations with some reference to giving back to your female friends everything that you receive from them. "It's a joy to be able to make a man happy, to know he appreciates you, to just do little things to please him and, of course, to be supportive in major ways. But giving to a woman, emotionally and materially, giving your time, your advice, etc., is extremely satisfying, too."

Now, considering all these benefits of good female friendships, what is it that keeps many women from getting the most out of friendship with other women? Why are so many women letting themselves miss out in this area?

Laura, a thirty-year-old, recently married patient, exemplifies one attitude that frequently keeps women from befriending other women. "My husband is my best friend," Laura says. "I don't need any other friends."

This sounds like an enviable situation, doesn't it? To have romance and friendship all in one person? But what is not so wonderful is carrying this concept so far, as Laura has, that you expect this male person to fulfill *all* your emotional and social needs.

When you look to this one person as your primary or only source of companionship, comfort, diversion, intellectual stimulation, etc., you tend to let other possible friendships slide. You make little or no attempt to form new friendships—not on your own, anyway.

In the long run—which is often not as long as we might think—the romantic ideal of lover/best friend often backfires on us, just as other romantic ideals do. For one thing, the expectation that a man is your only emotional and social support places an enormous burden on him and, therefore, on the relationship.

Secondly, should the relationship end, you've backed yourself into a rather isolated situation. Few women cut off all ties to the outside world as the result of having a lover/best friend to lean on. But through undervaluing your other relationships, you often find they're not all they could be when you do decide you need them.

As for single women who are looking for a lover/best friend and expect the man to support them emotionally—the tendency to shun other, potentially rewarding friendships along the way is, in fact, denying yourselves a great source of solace and sustenance in the here and now. This reinforces your loneliness and enhances your desperation to find Mr. Right.

Often, single women will avoid female friendships because they fear that heavy association with women will actually hinder them from finding Mr. Right. Laura, for instance, told me that before she met the man she married, she felt "funny" going to parties in the company of several female friends, or going to a movie with a woman, or going out to lunch or dinner or even for drinks with women she worked with who could have become friends.

"I guess I thought that, first of all, in environments where I might have met some eligible man, the fact that I was with women, or a woman, might discourage a man from approaching me—or even noticing me, singling me out.

"People do sometimes regard two women together or a group of three or four women together as kind of spinster types. And even if you're the most popular thing in your secretarial pool, and you know this, you can't help but feel as if people are pitying you, looking at you strangely, when you're in exclusively female company.

"And what if the man of your dreams is among the people pitying you? He might notice you from across the room, but he thinks, since you're with all these women, that there must be something wrong with you. I guess this was more or less the way I thought—so I never did have many close friendships with women."

I often hear, from women, that "I just can't seem to make friends with women" or "My friends aren't much comfort to me" or "The whole world's ignoring me." And, almost always, behind such proclamations is the deeply rooted belief that female friendship, in the hierarchy of emotional support systems, is a poor second to true love.

My feminist friends are fond of talking about the gentle, tolerant, peace-loving, nurturing qualities of women. Women, they say, have these traits in greater abundance than men do. If women ruled the world, they say, there would be no war. This may well be true. It is certainly poetic. And poets, too, have rhapsodized about the kindness, humanity, compassion of the female sex.

But I often wonder where this fine sensitivity is when women are relating not to men, children, pets, and the suffering masses—but to other women, women they know, women they work with, women they call their friends.

Sisterhood could be powerful. As it now stands, however, women are too frequently more competitive than cooperative. And I don't think the little skirmishes we wage with one another, overtly or otherwise, stem from genuine maliciousness or meanness or pettiness.

I think insecurity is responsible for most lapses in sisterhood—the fear that there are not enough men to go around, the fear that jobs are hard to come by, and the fear that all too few women will make it to the top so why not resent the existence of anyone who appears to be vying with you for top honors—or even standing in your way?

In fact, as I have pointed out, there are not enough men to go around. And good jobs are hard to come by, especially for women. But regarding other women as

the enemy is not going to solve either the man short-
age or the dearth of job opportunities.

And, in fact, should another woman "get" a man
you like or land a job you want, there is no reason to
regard her luck or achievement as a direct affront to
you, or as a taking-away of what is rightfully yours.

The woman who says "she stole him away from
me" or "she took the job I deserved" is not accusing
the woman who got the man or the job so much as she
is indicting herself—of being a self-centered individual who is unable to enjoy another person's enjoyment, to wish another person well, to avoid equating
what another person has with what she doesn't have.

Let me tell you, by way of example, the story of
Pamela and Carl and Cindy. Pamela and Cindy were
roommates and best friends. They had both come to
New York from smaller cities to "make it" as models.
Both were enjoying a moderate amount of success, in
their profession and in their social lives. Then Pamela
went to Haiti on location, and on the plane coming
back to New York she met Carl, a prosperous stock-
broker who had been to Haiti to obtain a quickie
divorce.

Pamela and Carl hit it off on the plane—so well that
they went straight from Kennedy Airport to the Plaza
Hotel where they spent three rapturous days and
nights. Then real life intruded (it always does). Both
Pamela and Carl had to get back to work.

Pamela returned to the apartment she shared with
Cindy. She was in a state of euphoria. She told Cindy
that she had met the man of her dreams, and Cindy
rejoiced with her. But when Carl arrived the following

night to take Pamela to dinner, Cindy's mood changed. She felt a strong attraction to Carl, and that upset her. Carl "belonged" to Pamela.

When the phone rang the next day, and it was Carl, Cindy told him to "Wait a minute—I'll get Pam." But Carl said, "No. Actually I was calling to talk to you."

Carl was confused, he told Cindy. He knew that Pamela was crazy about him. But he had thought, even initially, that she was "not his type." He liked her, but he was not interested in pursuing a romance with her. He wondered if Cindy would have dinner with him—and they could discuss what he should do.

So Cindy went to dinner with Carl. And to make a long story short, it turned out that her attraction to him was mutual. Carl's problem, of course, was now also mutual: How were Cindy and Carl going to break the news to Pamela that not only was Carl not about to declare his undying love for her—but he and Cindy had discovered they were soulmates.

Carl decided to be a gentleman and assume the entire burden of bearer-of-bad-tidings. Pamela took the news graciously. She understood, she told him. She appreciated his honesty. Thank God he had called a halt to the affair before she really got involved—and vulnerable.

But Pamela's attitude toward Cindy was not so gracious. "How could you *do* this to me?" she screamed. "The minute my back is turned you seduce the man I love! You knew how I felt! How could you take him away from me?"

Cindy reiterated what Carl had already told Pamela—that he liked her enormously as a friend and didn't want to lose her friendship. It was just that he didn't feel . . . *that way* about her, and he didn't want to lead her on, knowing how she felt.

"I didn't *take him!*" Cindy protested. "He called me to talk about you, if you want to know. He was terribly concerned about not hurting you. And then—we were just drawn to each other. You know. I can't explain it; we're just right together."

But Pamela wouldn't listen. As far as she was concerned, her roommate and best friend had betrayed her, had "stolen" something precious to her. She moved out of the apartment. She vowed never to speak to Cindy—or Carl—again.

So Pamela actually stole something from herself—a valued friendship (Cindy) and a potential friend (Carl). Pamela's overreaction stemmed from several erroneous assumptions (all having to do with her desperate dependence on male approval):

1. That a love relationship with a man is always far more rewarding than friendship with a woman.
2. If I don't land this terrific guy, I'll never find another one this terrific—there are so few of them around.
3. It is possible for one human being to steal another human being away from a third human being. In other words, loving someone is tantamount to owning him. He's property.

It would have been so much better, all around, if Pamela had been able to analyze the situation realistically. She could have concluded:

1. "Well, if Carl wasn't irresistibly drawn to me the way I was to him, it's a good thing I found out now!" (This is what she told Carl; but she didn't, apparently, believe it.)

2. "When you get down to it, he and I really didn't have that much in common. If he and Cindy have 'that certain something,' the more power to them!"

3. "I'm glad Cindy found someone so right for her. I hope I get lucky too, sometime."

Many of my patients, when I tell them this story or a similar story—say, of a wife whose husband skips off with another woman—think that it is absolutely ridiculous to imagine that the "abandoned" party could wish her "rival" well. And maybe, in some situations, that's true.

But in the interests of self-preservation, any woman, no matter what the situation, would be better off never viewing herself as "abandoned" (which implies "helpless," "cast-off," "rejected," "adrift") or as the victim of theft.

A woman who pivots around her own inner core of security, rather than being the satellite of a man, cannot feel bereft because of the luck or happiness of others.

Now let's look at a parallel situation—in the job market. Here, too, the overreliance on people and circumstances outside yourself for your feelings of self-worth can hamper your chances for female friendship.

What if, for example, you and a female co-worker, who happened to be your best friend, were up for the same job promotion. And she got it.

It would be natural for you to be disappointed. First of all, you missed out on the prestige, the step up the ladder of success, that the promotion signified. Secondly, you could have used the raise the promotion provided.

But your disappointment might go deeper. You might think, "This must mean she's better than I am. Probably I'll never get anywhere." In this case, you resent your friend—which can end, or considerably strain, the friendship. And you also put yourself down.

You blame her. ("She stole the job that should've been mine.") And at the same time you take her promotion as proof that you weren't qualified for it in the first place.

Wouldn't it be more constructive to drop the assumptions and analyze the facts? By acting on your assumptions, your resentment will inevitably come between you and your newly promoted friend. Why not look realistically at possible reasons that she moved ahead at this particular time and you didn't:

1. Maybe favoritism was involved. Maybe the boss, for reasons having nothing to do with you or your ultimate and intrinsic value as a human being, simply likes her.

2. Maybe she has special skills or knowledge that you lack.

3. Maybe the promotion had to do with the way she presents herself socially or the fact that she

has made more of an effort, socially, than you have. Getting ahead sometimes has as much or more to do with whom you know than how well you do your work.

4. Maybe the powers-that-be considered her appearance very compatible with the company's image and therefore put her in a higher visibility role to make the public statement that the company is as chic as its representative.

And there could be any number of other reasons. But what is important for you to understand is that, first, you are disappointed. And that's natural. But— the fact that your friend got the job does not make you incompetent or less of a person. It does not degrade you. It does not mean your friend is better than you.

What her promotion means is that the vicissitudes of life ended up in her favor, in this instance, rather than yours.

And now you can think of ways in which you can make life's vicissitudes operate in your favor next time:

1. Maybe, if you've figured out that your friend does have some skill or quality or even taste in clothes that you deem necessary for your own advancement, you could emulate her in this respect. Maybe you could ask her to help you improve yourself. Letting her know you admire her and asking her advice and assistance would certainly be much more beneficial to the friendship than seething with resentment of her.

2. By avoiding a breach of friendship, you may, in the long run, benefit from her advancement.

She may be in a position to help you get a promotion now or in the future. Continuing to be her good friend, someone she can confide in and come to for ideas and advice, could be productive in terms of your own career.

A woman who pivots around her own inner core of security does not consider other women a threat and does not pit herself against other women in a job situation.

She is able to be happy for a friend who has gotten ahead.

She does not automatically think, "Her gain is my loss."

She is able to enjoy her friend's enjoyment, in this and in other respects.

Being able to enjoy another person's enjoyment makes you a better friend. And it makes for better friendships.

"Fine!" many of my patients tell me when I point out how valuable female friendship can be in mitigating dependence on one special man for psychological sustenance. "You're right!" they say when I tell them how important it is get over cutthroat competitiveness, however subliminal, in order to form and maintain these friendships.

"But competition isn't my problem," my patients often go on to say. "My problem is that I am a good friend, but my friends always fall short of my expectations. Maybe I have the wrong friends or something.

Other people get invited to parties all the time, get cute postcards in the mail. Their friends call all the time. My friends just aren't as caring—or sharing—as they should be!"

Gwen, a twenty-six-year-old patient, felt this way. "There I was, lying in bed with the flu," she said, "and nobody called and asked, 'Can I bring you some chicken soup?' 'Can I do anything?' Nobody even called to say, 'Hi, I was worried about you. How are you?'"

"Did you tell anyone you were sick?" I asked Gwen.

"No, but they should've called anyway. Both Susan and Nancy, my two closest friends—both of them owed me a call . . ."

So Gwen languished, burning up more with righteous indignation than with fever, suffering more from her assumption that her friends didn't care about her than from the flu. As it turned out, Susan's two-year-old also had flu—so she was preoccupied with him. And Nancy, who was in graduate school, had exams.

Each of them was under the impression that Gwen "owed" her a call.

This sort of standoff—"Well, I'm not going to call her; it's her turn" or "I just had her over to dinner so now she should invite me"—happens frequently in friendships. And this attitude—that friendship is supposed to be a commodity consisting of equal parts of give and take which should be parceled out according to who owes whom—is the main reason that people so often feel slighted or forgotten or ignored by their "inconsiderate" friends.

This is yet another way in which we victimize ourselves with supposed-to thinking. Believing that friends are supposed to call you X number of times a week and remember your birthday in some creative and/or expensive way and invite you to every party they have is tantamount to, and no more enlightened than, believing that people who are happily married must make love X number of times a week and that unless you have X number of orgasms per lovemaking session, your sex life is a failure.

I said to Gwen, "Why don't you call your friends up and say, 'I'm down in the dumps because I'm sick' and have a little conversation and then, before hanging up, say, 'Why don't you call later? When I'm not feeling well, I really crave attention.'"

"I could never do that," said Gwen. "They're supposed to think of that themselves. It's just good manners."

"What if they never read Emily Post?" I asked.

One of the cardinal rules of friendship in my book is that there are no rules. That means that just because you are a certain way and do certain things, you shouldn't expect other people, who have been brought up differently and have different values, to conform to your ways of thinking and acting.

And when they don't live up to your supposed-to's, don't assume that:

1. They don't care about me, and—

2. There must be something wrong with me because they don't care about me.

Instead, cool all those expectations. Never judge other people by the same exact standards according to which you operate.

And don't "rebel" by vowing "I swear I won't call her until she calls me."

If you call her more than she calls you, that doesn't mean she is not holding up her end so much as it is a tribute to your generosity, your good breeding, your talent for friendship. You should feel proud, if anything—not bitter.

Good friends do not think in terms of tit for tat. A primary quality of solid friendship is, in fact, that months and even years can elapse between get-togethers and even between phone conversations—and when you and this dear friend do, finally, make contact, it's as if you just spoke yesterday.

I have this kind of relationship with some of my college chums who are now scattered all over the globe, making frequent reunions impossible.

A patient of mine described this kind of relationship with a friend of hers who lives in the same city she does. Yet their respective, furiously busy lives preclude their seeing each other or talking on the phone as much as they'd like: "Emily understands that I'm tied up with my career," my patient told me. "I understand that she is tied up with her husband, her two young daughters, her two households, and the property she and her husband own. She's the one who manages the real estate.

"Since she has even more preoccupations than I do, I'm the one who really makes the effort to keep in contact. I call her. I'm the one who says, 'Hey, if you can get out from under, let's have lunch this week.'

"Sometimes, I get so wrapped up in the logistics of my own life that I don't call her for months at a stretch—and she doesn't call me. But then, when we do get together, we have so much to tell each other, and we communicate as intimately as ever.

"And I know, even during our periods of separation, that should I ever need to cry on someone's shoulder at three A.M. or need a loan or need to go camp out at her house or need anything, I can call her. And she knows she can call me, too, anytime, for anything.

"Just this knowledge keeps me from ever feeling isolated or empty or lonely."

A friend of mine has a placard on her desk that says, "You can never be too rich or too thin." If I adopted a similar slogan, it might be: "You can never have too many friends."

It is to every woman's advantage to expand her circle of female friends, her own personal sisterhood, as much as possible.

Yet many patients complain that they find it difficult to make new friends. Or they show a marked reluctance, even laziness, in this area.

I find that their "difficulties," or hesitation about making friends, usually does not stem from unwillingness but rather from fear.

Just as you can be afraid to be alone, you can be afraid of other people. Often, I find both fears in one person, because the two fears are related. They come from the same place—a shaky self-image, too much dependence on outside elements for your well-being.

Leah, who is thirty, unmarried, and very beautiful, complained to me that she can't seem to make new friends easily. "I'll go to a party," she said, "and nobody ever comes up to me. Nobody seeks me out. I guess I just don't look attractive enough, or fascinating. I just don't have what it takes."

Leah is right, in a way. But not in the way that she thinks. The problem is not her looks, certainly. The problem is that Leah, like lots of other women I know, operates according to several erroneous assumptions about what life at a party is actually like.

First of all, Leah assumes that the majority of people at parties case the joint, pick out some scintillating-looking person, and then go up and befriend that person.

Not so. The fact is, most people at parties do just what Leah does. They wait. They wait for someone to find them fascinating and talk to them. Sometimes, while they wait, they talk to someone they already know. Then, after a certain amount of time has elapsed, and their life has not been enriched by some dazzling new friend wandering into it, they go home thinking, "What a downer that party was." Or, "I must be losing my touch."

Leah has another erroneous assumption about parties. She's always read, in magazines and novels, about these women who have the ability to walk into a roomful of otherwise occupied people and cause all conversation, drinking, and munching of hors d'oeuvres to stop. "Who *is* she?" everyone murmurs as they fall all over one another to meet her.

Now, I'm not going to go out on a limb and say that the phenomenon of the woman who causes all eyes to become riveted to her just by walking into the room never happens, or that it happens only in fiction. But in my entire life—and that includes more parties than I'll admit to—I have seen it happen only once.

I was at a get-together given by a prominent actor. And into his mobbed and smoky loft walked this woman who must have been six feet tall. She had electric blue hair. She was wearing what looked very much like one of those bags the dry-cleaning comes back in—plastic and clear. And, indeed, upon her appearance, every single person in that room stopped whatever they were doing and stared.

Furthermore, everyone did want to know who she was—wouldn't you? (It turned out that she was the lead singer in an all-female punk-rock band.)

The point is, if Leah—or you—want to steal any given scene that badly, the punk-rock lady is one act you can follow. You can make yourself exotic and freaky—and some people will try to make your acquaintance.

But the majority of people won't. They might try to find out who you are, and why you're got up that way, but they might, in fact, be intimidated—and avoid you.

This happens to absolutely gorgeous women, too, by the way. These are women who you might imagine, because they look so exquisite, would magnetize people. But that's not the way things work. Often, great beauty intimidates rather than attracts.

So what I suggested to Leah is that what it takes to be magnetic and mesmerizing—what she thinks she lacks—is simply the nerve to go up to another person and start a conversation. Why not be one of the few people who make the contacts? When you walk into a roomful of people, look them over, see who appears to be the most interesting-looking person, male or female, in the crowd, and introduce yourself.

"What if they're talking to someone else?" Leah asked.

"Then kind of hang around a bit and wait until there's a pause in the conversation and *then* introduce yourself."

"But isn't that rude?" Leah wanted to know.

"No. I wouldn't find it rude. I'd find it delightful."

"But wouldn't it be intrusive? And what if they ignored me or put me down? I remember one time I went to this press party for a singer I was dying to meet. I kept watching her, and she kept talking to her friends. Finally, I went up to her and hovered while she and this other woman conducted this heavy conversation. And finally, they noticed me standing there and just looked at me like I was some kind of disease. I was mortified. I never want to risk that happening again."

Leah concluded that the two women's indifference to her must have been her fault: "I guess they didn't think I looked hip enough to get to know."

Leah had never considered that there might have been other explanations, having nothing to do with her, until I suggested some of them: The women could have been discussing private matters. They could have been gossiping—again, private business. They could have been drunk. They could have been talking business. They could have been nearsighted.

In any case, the constructive thing to do when someone does not respond to your interest is to find the next-most-fascinating person in the room and open a conversation and see what happens.

Look upon it not as leaving yourself open, repeatedly, for rejection—but as an adventure. You're in control. You're choosing them. Sometimes, tenacity is in order.

It should be clear that both the quantity and quality of your female friendships can vastly enrich your life, serving as a source of companionship and comfort that can act as a buffer against loneliness and can augment, or even substitute for, a relationship with a man.

The quality of your friendships can be greatly enhanced by solidifying this support system into a real group, serving as a catalyst for other women to get to know one another.

In the working world, women have a valuable resource in the process of networking, sharing contacts, using contacts they have to make more contacts.

But women have not yet made such great, cooperative strides socially, or in terms of emotionally supporting one another. Social networking or life-style networking is something that any woman can do among her own friends, in her own community or city.

Let me give you an example. Linda is a thirty-five-year-old patient whose husband divorced her quite suddenly, leaving her with two small children to raise. Linda had always had a group of female friends with whom she was close. She had known some of these women since her college days. During her marriage, she had let some of these friendships lapse—or the contact remained, but the closeness had diminished.

Linda, recognizing that she needed good company and an understanding audience from time to time, and conjecturing that her friends could use the same thing, organized the Saturday Night Club. She called all the women she had been close to, as well as current "best friends," and invited them to join this group which would meet once a week or more—not necessarily on Saturday nights. The name only derived from the fact that Saturday night has come to be a social symbol, the night when anyone without a date is supposed to feel especially low.

The members of the Saturday Night Club are both married and single. Although, sometimes, the conversation at the get-togethers resembles that of a group therapy session, the tone of the average meeting ranges from joke telling to political debates to exchanging recipes. The content sort of happens; the idea is merely companionship, being surrounded by caring friends, making new friends—because, as women introduce new members to the group, the club is growing to the point that Linda jokes, "Soon we're going to have to rent Lincoln Center for our meetings."

Despite the Saturday Night Club's social thrust, its informality, the group is well enough organized that if a member has a personal crisis, she can call an "emergency meeting" for therapeutic talk and comfort.

The Food Group is another example of friendship formalized—this time, around a special interest, international cuisines. It was started by Toni, a woman whose parents, when she was growing up, had a gourmet club—four couples who met once a month for a gala dinner comprised of the national specialties of one foreign country.

Each couple would research and make one or two dishes—so each meal was a cooperative method, Toni recalls. "I think that by the time I was sixteen they had circled the globe twice—from New Orleans to Sri Lanka!"

Toni decided that there was no reason why she and her female friends, including two who are married and whose husbands would eat nothing more exotic than steak and hamburger, couldn't do what these couples did. And The Food Group has been very rewarding, not only as an excuse to socialize but in terms of culinary education.

There are infinite possibilities for special interest groups—poetry reading, theatergoing, putting on plays yourself, yoga, calisthenics, hiking, biking.

And life-style networking can extend to living arrangements, too. Maggie Kuhn, the head of the Gray Panthers, lives in a house with many other people, both men and women—an extended family. Communal living, of course, is not for everyone. But it is a solution for some single people who feel isolated, particularly in urban areas where the sense of neighborhood, of "extended family," is often hard to come by.

What I do recommend for any single woman who is lonely and, perhaps, under financial pressure, is to find a roommate—not only for companionship but to share expenses.

I know of several instances where single mothers with young children paired up, obtained bigger apartments than they could otherwise afford, and shared not only the cost of living but child-raising and baby-sitting responsibilities.

When one goes out, the other looks after the children. The problem of both women working is easily resolved since, with two salaries, a babysitter is affordable. Or the women work different shifts, so that whoever is at home does the baby-sitting.

Increasingly, women are roommating with men, too.

Nonsexual relationships with men are not only possible but can become an integral part of any extramarital or extraromantic life-support system—as you will see in the next chapter.

VI
Man: A Woman's Best Friend

Friendships with men can be as intimate, relaxed, and emotionally sustaining as your friendships with women—in new and surprising ways.

A man need not be your lover to be a "best friend."

And if a man with whom you have a close friendship should become your lover, this fact need not take the nonjudgmental, unpossessive, no-need-to-impress-him quality out of the relationship.

Furthermore, being good friends with a number of men significantly reduces desperate dependence on that one special man or desperation to find one.

I have been lucky enough to have several male friends who are like "girlfriends"—we can discuss our innermost thoughts and feelings without inhibitions that arise from sexual role playing. They don't yawn and excuse themselves if I bring up some trivia that is on my mind—such as: "Should I get my hair cut?" or "What do you think I should do with this room?"

And my men friends listen nonjudgmentally to my fears, worries, problems, and irrational gripes—and I do the same for them.

Many patients ask, "How do you find men like that? I didn't know they existed!" I assure you, they exist. Then, too, there are plenty of men who don't know they have this potential to have a highly satisfying, platonic relationship with a woman.

And you can help them develop this potential—and help yourself to a good friend in the process.

What often keeps women from availing themselves of male friendship is the same assumption that so frequently causes trauma on dates and in relationships: that sex is foremost on men's minds.

Many women have told me, "I never had a relationship with a man that was nonsexual. I think sex is *always* an issue between men and women."

Sexual undertones often exist when a man meets a woman—but not always and inevitably. Furthermore, nowhere is it written that every sexual impulse you have, or someone else has, must be acted upon. A married patient of mine once told me that her "absolute best friend in the world" is the husband of one of her close friends.

She said, "When we met, there was an undeniable sexual spark between us. But there was also no question that I am madly in love with, and loyal to, my husband—and he feels the same way about his wife. So our friendship is totally nonsexual.

"But I think that the fact that we find each other attractive enhances our relationship. We both get ego gratification from it—Wow! Someone out there, who I'm not married to, thinks I'm irresistible! But on the whole, I really think of him and relate to him almost as if he were a girlfriend; and, to him, I'm a 'good buddy.'"

Male-female friendship often develops more easily if one party is happily married to or going with someone else—or if both already have successful romantic involvements. In this case, while mutual attraction may play a part in the formation of the friendship, sex itself does not become an issue. Romance does not distract the two friends from their intellectual or work-related or other type of rapport.

Mark, a bachelor who has many female friends with whom he's never had affairs, says that most of these women are living with or married to other men. "I don't try to become friends with married, as opposed to single, women," Mark says. "But I do find that the sort of easygoing, undemanding camaraderie that constitutes friendship with both men and women happens more frequently with women who are clearly in love with their husbands or boyfriends. Because the pressure's off. They categorically exclude the possibility of getting emotionally entangled with me—and vice versa. We can relax."

Mark, who is in no hurry to get married, finds that his friendships with women are even more satisfying on certain levels than his romantic involvements— "Because there's no game playing, because the expectations on both sides are not emotion-charged."

Furthermore, Mark gets platonically involved with women far more readily than he becomes emotionally involved. "My career is foremost on my mind right now," he says. "I can't afford the time and energy it takes to keep up, let alone establish, a serious love relationship.

"And I get enough moral support from my friends that I don't feel a crying need to fall in love—and by my friends I mean both women and men. Actually, I don't perceive too much difference between my female and male friends. Friends are friends."

Sam, a corporate lawyer who has been married for twelve years and has two young sons, shares Mark's assertion that gender has little or no importance in the quality of his friendships. "Even in my bachelor days," he says, "I really didn't have the attitude that women are 'different,' that because a person was female, I should base my interest on her sexual attractiveness. My friendships with women have always come about because of the sharing of interests other than sex.

"For instance, I'd become pals with colleagues. And some of my friendships with women evolved from a mutual passion for silversmithing, my hobby. Libby, for instance, is a silversmithing buddy. It seems to me that when I talk to her, I don't talk differently than I do with Pete, who silversmiths with me and is a close friend of mine. There's no difference in the quality of the conversation. With both my men and women friends it's the same revealing of feelings, attitudes, sensibilities—and the exchange of ideas and opinions."

There are many men who are as open to being "just friends" with women as Mark and Sam are.

But, judging from what my female patients say, the men *they* seem to run into all the time lend credence to the women's assumption that men are, first and foremost, looking for sex when they strike up an acquaintance with a woman.

As I mentioned earlier, men often "come on" to women because they think that's what women expect, because they're playing their male role to the hilt. And often, underneath that macho front, there's a sensitive, thoughtful person who would make a good friend.

But here are some of the things that might happen when a woman wants to be "just friends" with a man, and he makes it clear that he wants to be her lover:

1. She rebuffs him in no uncertain terms; he retreats, rejected. All chances of any relationship are cut off.

2. She says no, but nicely enough so that he assumes there is sexual interest on her part and that if he keeps trying, he'll win her over. Thus a relationship is in the making—but it does not have the makings of open, easygoing friendship.

3. She decides to sleep with him against her own better judgment. In this case, a wonderful, soul-satisfying, platonic friendship is not usually in the offing—although some sexual relationships do lead to the man and woman becoming great pals after the romance has waned.

Male-female friendships are no more able to be sliced into predictable categories or shaped by general principles than any other area of human relations.

But let me tell you about three cases of men and women becoming lifelong platonic friends—*after* they had resolved the issue of sex.

Eileen, who teaches political science, and Phil, an editor of a political journal, met at a party and, from Eileen's description, they struck up quite a substantial discussion about foreign affairs before heading to Phil's apartment to begin an affair of their own. (Or so each of them assumed the other thought.)

"But I didn't really like Phil *that way*," Eileen recalls. "I don't know why we ended up in bed together. We had both had one too many, and I guess it seemed to be the appropriate modern boy-meets-girl thing to do. Anyway, I remember suffering through the whole love scene, you know. Because I just wasn't turned on by him. There was just none of that chemistry. But he was such a nice guy! How could I say no?

"And then, once we had done the deed, how could I tell him how I honestly felt? He obviously had had a lot more fun than I had!"

Nevertheless, Eileen managed, on her next date with Phil, to circumvent the issue of sex. She told him that even though she found him very attractive, she was still "hung up" on her ex-boyfriend and was not ready for a physical involvement. "Couldn't we just be friends for the time being?" she asked Phil. "I like you so much."

To Eileen's surprise, Phil was extremely understanding. He liked her, too, he told her, adding that he felt relieved, because he wasn't prepared to make a commitment either. In his experience, sex led to commitment. He welcomed the idea of "just hanging out together."

It has been three years since Eileen and Phil began "hanging out." They have not become lovers. Each has helped the other through romances with other people.

"If it weren't for the emotional support I get from Phil," Eileen says, "I know I would've fallen into some big romance with one of the many guys I've dated and been turned on by—but who weren't right for me—just out of the need to have a male presence in my life. Phil, and a couple of other men friends, have saved me from mistaking sexual attraction for love more than once."

In Margot's case, she and the man who has been her best friend for the last four years started out as more than a one-night stand. They were married to each other for two years.

"Richard and I fell in love during our senior year in high school," Margot explains. "We were an item all through college. He was an English lit. major; he wrote poems for me. I guess I thought he was like a latter-day Lord Byron. We got married three months after graduating from college. He wanted to be a writer, but we couldn't live on the meager income he got from the occasional poem or short story he sold. We depended mostly on my income." (Margot worked, at the time, as a design apprentice in a major fashion house. She now has her own line of ready-to-wear with the same company.)

"But Richard couldn't stand 'sponging off' me, as he put it. So he went to work for his father's furniture manufacturing company. He stopped writing and became all business. I lost all respect for him; I thought he had sold out. But that wasn't the reason our marriage ground to a halt. I thought it was, but in retrospect I see—we both see—that we were too young. We hadn't developed our own goals or even our own personalities, really. So we couldn't very well form mutual goals and a life-style, right?

"Anyway, I initiated the divorce. Richard went along with it, but not without considerable bitterness. At one point, he actually told me he hated me; I had ruined his life.

"So we went our separate ways, with no communication for a while. I was moving ahead in my career. And Richard was doing very well, totally overhauling his father's rather moribund company with adaptations, shall we say, of the latest styles from Milan.

"Then one day we bumped into each other on the street. My office was in the same neighborhood as his—I suppose it was inevitable. He asked me to have a drink, and I was rushing off somewhere, so I took a rain check. About a week later, we did get together for drinks. And it was like old home week. We had so much to talk about. First of all, our respective careers—each of us was proud of the other's success.

"But above and beyond that, we had a common history. We grew up together, really, and we had all these friends in common, memories of vacations we took, the smell of hamburgers cooking on the grill on a summer evening in his father's backyard years and years ago.

"It was painful and it was poignant. And we both realized how much we'd been missing by avoiding each other. By this time, he was involved with the woman he later married. She was in the furniture business, too. He had met her in Italy. And I was having an affair with my boss. I thought it would be forever, but history, of course, proved me wrong.

"Anyway, we shared something that his fianceé and my lover couldn't ever possibly share, a common past, the way we were—right? I was the only one in the world who knew that Richard, this prosperous-looking man in the three-piece suit, whose conversation now revolved around his latest stock market coup and his new car was, at heart, a poet. And I guess he had a hotline to my soul, too: He knew that inside the little fashion designer—me!—was a would-be Georgia O'Keeffe, yearning for a one-woman show at the Museum of Modern Art.

"Richard and I now talk on the phone at least twice a week and see each other often. He's just become a father for the first time, and I've just become engaged.

"And every so often we flirt, kind of, but basically I couldn't conceive of being romantically involved with him, at this point, and the feeling's undoubtedly mutual. And yet we're closer than we would have been had we stayed married. In many ways, he's just as precious to me as Gerry, my fiancé. I could almost say that if something happened and I didn't marry Gerry, I'd survive; I wouldn't be thrilled, of course, but I'd manage."

Derek and Gail were never lovers. But he, at least, had that in mind at the outset of their relationship.

Gail, twenty-eight, is a film editor. She met Derek when she was working on a project for his small production company, which specializes in television commercials.

"Derek hit on me immediately," Gail recalls, "and I was flattered—and tempted to go out with him. Who wouldn't have been? He's a real Whiz Kid—thirty-two and he's got his own production company, turning out really hip commercials. He's not rich yet—all his money goes back into the business. But he's really gonna make it someday. *And* he looks just like Warren Beatty.

"The trouble was, he also acted like Warren Beatty—in *Shampoo*. His smug, almost plastic, self-assurance as he pursued me put me on my guard. He was not so much asking me for a date as just asking me to name the time and place, since he assumed the date was a *fait accompli*. Of course, I'd go out with him. He had but to snap his fingers and every woman within a radius of ten miles came running!

"So I thought, 'Uh-oh. This guy's trouble. Any woman who falls for him is in for a real hard time.' But I suspected—and I was right, as it turned out—that underneath Derek's carefully cultivated lover-boy facade, he was really the boy next door, you know?

"His commercials showed real understanding of people. They were—and are—highly sensitive little documentaries. So I thought anybody who can put all that feeling into what is essentially a plug for a product has got to have some depth to him.

150 °

"So I made a real attempt to draw him out. We talked a lot in the course of working together and, after a while, he dropped the lover-boy act and started being himself—in short, a man who was afraid of involvement and avoided it in the usual, casebook way, with lots of hit-and-run action.

"Derek didn't really understand anything about women and, frankly, he didn't understand himself too well, either. His whole life-style was one of avoiding confrontations with either his true self or the people inside all the beautiful bodies he seduced and abandoned.

"The way I drew Derek out was to confide in him, to behave with him not as if he were the star-of-*Shampoo* clone he wanted me to think he was, but as the nice, vulnerable person I suspected he was. I told him about my various romantic fiascoes. I asked his advice about this guy I was dating on and off. I talked about my professional goals and asked his advice about what I could do to really stand out from the hundreds of other film editors running around New York.

"He was extremely responsive. The poor guy really hadn't let down his defenses for so long, maybe for his whole life, that my true confessions game—at least it started as a game—came as an enormous relief to him. He didn't have any real, solid, sincere friendships. He had left his old childhood and college friends behind, eclipsed them, felt superior to them. The women he knew he regarded as objects, truly. His men friends were of the clap-'em-on-the-back-and-talk-business ilk.

"Derek and I now have a relationship that's like the buddy system at summer camp. With him around, I'm never afraid of drowning—and vice versa. Just recently, he said to me, 'You know, you're the only woman who's ever rejected me sexually that I ever spoke to again. You're the only woman friend I ever had. And listen, kid, I wouldn't sleep with you on a bet now—so don't try anything—because that would ruin our beautiful friendship!'"

Gail laughed when she told me Derek's remark. But I know quite a few women who wouldn't find it so funny, if it had been directed at them.

One of the reasons that some women have a hard time being "just friends" with men is not so much that they assume, rightly or wrongly, that sex is all that's on men's minds. In some cases, the obstacle to friendship is that sex is very much on the woman's mind. She wants the man to want her sexually—if only for ego gratification. *Her* ego is on the line. She relies, for her sense of self-worth, on knowing that this man is panting with desire for her and then, once she's satisfied his desire, that he will stick around, demonstrating his on-going passion.

In other words, a leading reason that women are unable to be "just friends" with men, thereby acquiring a means of deflecting their dependence on True Love and Modern Romance, is that they regard every acceptable man that comes along as a candidate for True Love and Modern Romance.

What, exactly, are the qualities that make friendship with a man worthwhile? Several women who count men among their best friends made the following points:

1. "I learn different things from men than I do from female friends. I don't mean this to sound sexist—but men do have interests that are different from ours. For instance, fishing. I know very few women who are ardent anglers.

"But Jack, one of my men friends, took me fishing recently, and I caught a red snapper and I was hooked, so to speak. I go every weekend now—sometimes with him, sometimes with people I met through him. It's a whole new world. I read books on marine biology. Jack really expanded my horizons."

2. "My male friends have clued me in to what could be called 'the masculine mystique.' What I mean is, through conversations with them, through hearing their problems and asking them to help me wrestle with my problems, I've learned lots about the way men think and feel. Getting the male point of view on various issues, which can be anything from whether I can improve my driving a car around a curve to the sexual prudishness of my latest boyfriend—is useful, enlightening, and comforting."

3. "You're never hard up for a date when you've got men friends. I've found, over and over, that I can enjoy myself as much with a man I just like as with a man I love. Romance is not a prerequisite for good conversation, cracking jokes, sneer-

ing together at some lousy movie you made the mistake of seeing, trying the strange food at the new Ethiopian restaurant—all the things that make for good company, a well-spent evening or afternoon."

4. "I'll tell you what I get from my men friends that I don't get from women. A feeling of being protected. For instance, the comfort you get from a woman friend is maternal, warm, emotional fortitude. I'm not saying men can't be maternal, etc. They can. But men, just by being physically bigger or more muscular or just by being male, give you a kind of protective comfort. I think this has to do with my admittedly old-fashioned connection of maleness with authority, too. The father image.

"Whatever the reasons, I can give you a very good example of what I'm talking about. I had a serious operation a few years ago. As I came out of the anesthesia, I became aware of my family and close friends in the room. And I love every one of those people—but the ones I reached for, the ones I wanted to hold my hand, were my husband and Bobby, my business partner, who's also been a dear friend for years."

Another advantage of being "just friends" with a man is that it's a good practice for what we consider "the real thing." It's like a test run.

Tapping the friendship potential of men is a good way to find out what the natural, mutual dependence that makes for a great love relationship is all about.

He depends on you for comfort, advice, a pep talk. And vice versa. He can call you at three in the morning and say, "I can't sleep. I've got to talk." And vice versa. It's a two-way street. It's symbiotic—and yet there's nothing desperately dependent or clinging about it—unless, of course, you've chosen a raving neurotic for a friend, in which case you might suggest to him that going into therapy might prove more fruitful than anything you can tell him at three A.M. over the phone.

Another thing about non-clinging dependence between friends is that should you, for instance, call him and he is unable to listen to you pour your heart out, he can say, "Listen, I'm on my way out the door—but if you call back in two hours, I'm all yours. You know I understand how you feel, and I'm with you—so just hold on till I get back."

And you will feel buoyed by this—not rejected.

I have heard many stories of "just friends" relationships leading to "the real thing." And, in my experience, marriages or romances that evolved from solid friendships are more likely to work out than those sparked merely by initial physical involvement.

Maria and Paul were friends for several months before they became lovers. And they were lovers—and friends—for two years before they got married. Paul was a recent widower when he and Maria met at a mutual friend's wedding.

"We were introduced during the reception," Maria says, "and we liked each other instantly. Neither of us talked much to the other people at the reception because we seemed to have so much to say to each other. We continued the conversation after the reception over dinner at the best Spanish restaurant in town, according to Paul. And he was right. That was one mutual passion we discovered immediately—paella.

"As for the other kind of passion—Paul was still very much in mourning for his wife who had died around six months before we met. They were married for twenty-two years. He told me about his wife's death during our first evening together. He talked very openly about his loneliness and his feelings of inadequacy at being both a father and a mother to his two teenage daughters.

"Paul wasn't ready to become involved when we met, and I understood that and didn't pressure him. I didn't even feel inclined to pressure him, to tell you the truth, because my initial response to him wasn't romantic, like in the novels when the heroine feels her pulse quicken upon proximity to the hero.

"I guess, in restrospect, I was attracted to Paul in that I recognized that he had a distinguished face and a good build—although he was a little on the thin side then. Also, I think I sensed at the beginning that this was someone special.

"But I didn't go one step further and think, 'This is *the* someone special.' I thought that because he was different from any man I'd ever met, in that he gave me this feeling of total, nonjudgmental acceptance, he was someone I'd really like as a friend. I thought, 'What a *nice* man!'

"By the time we did make love, it was by common, unspoken consent. It just happened, one night, part of the natural flow of things. And there was none of the usual first-time shyness or clumsiness.

"We knew each other so well by then that the physical part was neither as dramatic nor as traumatic as it is between two near-strangers. It was, essentially, an act of friendship, a very precious expression of a cherished friendship.

"So I guess you could say that when I married Paul, I married my best friend."

Although the addition of sex to male-female friendship can enhance that friendship and turn it into a love affair, sex has also been known to have a negative effect on such friendships.

When the Warren Beatty look-alike said to Gail that he was afraid sex would "ruin our beautiful friendship," he was being facetious, but the prospect was not without precedent.

A patient of mine named Carol, a bright, twenty-five-year-old medical student, came to my office in tears one afternoon because she was so worried about her suddenly stormy relationship with Steve, also a medical student.

"Everything was wonderful," Carol told me. "We got along as if we had known each other forever. We had so much fun. Sex wasn't a big thing, you know. We were both so crazed with studying that who had time for sex? Besides we kept assuring each other that we were just best friends.

"Then Steve told me he loved me one afternoon in the middle of cramming for an exam. And I realized I loved him. So suddenly, we were both so crazed with sex that who had time for studying?

"It was fabulous for a while. But lately I've started getting really off the wall. I get antsy if he doesn't call on time. I suspect him of seeing other women. I want him to get a haircut so he can meet my parents, and he refuses to. I don't want to be so bitchy and demanding, but I can't seem to stop. And I can't concentrate on my work."

There are two possible explanations behind Carol's transformation from Steve's caring and compassionate friend to the mopey, lovelorn woman who arrived in my office that afternoon.

One possibility is that Carol may never truly have thought of Steve as "just a friend." She might have been playing the you're-my-best-friend game in order to land him. Then, once Steve opened his mouth and out came those three little words, Carol, operating according to all the assumptions we've debunked in previous chapters, felt she had license to expect and demand much more than she would from "just a friend."

The other possibility is that Carol and Steve were genuinely "just friends," as Carol claimed. But the minute sex entered into the picture, the natural give-and-take of their friendship became a business proposition—because Carol, and maybe Steve, too, attach many more supposed-to's to love/sex than to friendship.

When love is declared, it sometimes supersedes the fact of friendship. The relationship is now a game with lots of rules and a lot at stake.

A nonsexual relationship has fewer strings attached. If you are "just friends" with a man, and he calls and announces, "I'm engaged to Mary Lou!" your response would probably be, "Congratulations!" You would wish him well.

If, on the other hand, you are sleeping with this man and have come to expect an eventual commitment from him—and he, instead, makes a commitment to Mary Lou, you may not be so delighted.

As I explained to Carol, the only way to keep sexual involvement from eroding your friendship with a man is to see things as they really are: "Okay, now my friend and I have added sex to all the other things we have in common."

This realistic reading of the situation is far less risky emotionally than immediately concluding: "Okay. We've made love. Now he owes me . . ."

I wish more women would let themselves have comfortable, easy sexual friendships with men without considering or fretting about whether it is going to be permanent. Because this is the best possible trial run for "the real thing."

What is marriage, anyway, if not a comfortable, easy sexual friendship?

And what is a good marriage if not an opportunity to give as much as you get?

Our male friends stand to gain quite a bit from us, including, according to some of my own male friends:

1. "An overall better understanding of women."

2. "Someone I can talk to about things I can't discuss, or feel embarrassed about discussing, with other guys—like my fear over some medical problem, for example, or what to buy my wife

for her birthday, or some problem I'm having with my daughter."

3. "A sense of security and comfort that my male friends don't seem to exude. I noticed that after my wife died, the friends who really showed interest, called, invited me over, put up with my depressed state, were all women. The men weren't nearly as compassionate. My men friends couldn't listen at length to my discussing, for instance, my difficulties adjusting to life alone. But my woman friends could—and did."

4. "An opportunity to try and be more expressive of my feelings. I've always been lousy at saying what I really feel, what's really bothering me. Like most men, I never want to admit there's a crack in the armor. I'm leery of saying anything that would make me seem weak. But, through the women I know, I've come to realize that a weakness, here and there, is just human—it's not, or shouldn't be, mortifying. My women friends, through their openness have helped me to stop being afraid of myself—weak, childish, however I am at any given time."

I found that last statement especially intriguing. If more women started being friends with men in a nonaggressive, non-"I want to capture you" way, then more men would espouse the female-attributed qualities (showing emotion, exposing their weaknesses, admitting flaws) that are conducive to good, humane relations between the sexes.

If more women thought—and acted—in terms of making connections with men rather than clinching commitments, men would follow suit. The battle of the sexes would cease—because men and women would realize they're on the same side. And all of us would be winners!

VII
Money and Your Career: Becoming More Supportive of Yourself

We've seen how friendship can help deflect total reliance on one man for your emotional well-being. But supporting yourself financially—or contributing to your financial support—is vital, too, in overcoming desperate dependence.

Financial independence contributes to emotional undependence, because:

1. If you are single, earning your own living precludes being overly anxious to find a man to give you the life-style you want.

2. If you are involved with a man who provides for you financially, earning your own living will spring you from the trap of perpetual childhood: having to ask permission to spend his money. You will stop being on the dole, with him parceling out your weekly allowance. (It comes as a constant shock to me that in this day and age so many wives refer to the household budget as "my allowance.")

3. The more a woman pays her own way, the more self-esteem she has. Financial security goes a long way toward building your inner core of security.

4. The source of your income—your job—can be as fulfilling as love or friendship. I can't tell you how many women, married and single, have told me, "Work is my only salvation."

When I point out to my patients how rewarding work can be, psychologically and not just financially, they are often skeptical. "It sounds good," a patient recently said, "but let's be brutally realistic. You can't hold hands with your job. You can't curl up in bed with it. Nothing, including the greatest job in the world, is as satisfying as the love of a man."

This statement reminded me of a line in the film *All About Eve*. Bette Davis, playing an aging star whose love affair is in jeopardy, said: "In the final analysis, the only thing that matters is when you look up at six o'clock and there he is. Otherwise, you're nothing but something with a French provincial desk."

All About Eve was made in 1950. I find that women's underlying attitudes toward their jobs and careers haven't changed too much since then—despite all the media attention to women in the marketplace, despite financial columns in women's magazines, despite entire magazines such as *Savvy* and *Working Woman* that are directed at women with jobs and careers, despite for-men-only fields beginning to welcome women.

The degree to which women of all ages still let the fact that they are women (and the assumption that a woman cannot be fulfilled without being a wife and/or mother) take precedence over their identities (real or potential) as lawyers, CPA's, stockbrokers, editors, actresses, etc., is astounding.

When I ask my patients to explain why they do not work harder at making their jobs fulfilling, or why they don't try to earn more, or why they don't work at all, they often cite economic realities. "Even if I wanted to get ahead," a woman told me recently, "it's impossible."

It is true that surviving in the working world can be discouraging even to women who are single-mindedly determined to have brilliant careers. The job market definitely favors men. According to current statistics, for every dollar a man makes, a woman earns fifty-nine cents. Only one percent of all executives in the country are women.

Little wonder that a woman might conclude that her best bet in life is to hook a man and let him give her what she wants—or, at least, more than what she is capable of acquiring on her own.

But, ironically, this very attitude prevents women from acquiring more of an economic edge. So many women regard work as treading water until some man comes to the rescue. Or they take a job because the husband's salary is not sufficient, but with definite plans to retire and be taken care of the minute inflation disappears or the husband gets a substantial enough raise or when they win the sweepstakes.

So we're talking about a two-way street: Women lag behind men in earning power and power in general—but this is not entirely the fault of men or of society. It is partly women's fault, for not taking themselves seriously enough as professionals, as employees—as possible tycoons!

I've noticed that many of my patients have very well developed imaginations when it comes to their romantic interests. But in other respects, their imaginations are woefully limited; they go only so far. I am always hearing self-assessments along the following lines:

"I can imagine myself making my own living—but not for the rest of my life."

"I can imagine myself making my own living—but not getting rich *on my own*."

"I can imagine myself buying a sable coat should I happen to get rich on my own—but not buying a piece of real estate or dabbling in the stock market. I know this might make me richer, but I can't relate to real estate or stocks."

"I can imagine myself being vice-president of the company—but not president."

Many of my patients are held back not only by lack of imagination in terms of money and career potential. They also hold themselves back because they assume that by remaining virginal in financial matters and by making it clear to one and all that marriage (or, at least, love) outranks work in their scheme of things, they will be more attractive to men.

The idea seems to be, in the case of single women: "The more helpless I appear, the more likely it is that some man will want to provide for me."

And, in the case of women who live with men: "The more I can make him think of himself as my big, strong provider, the less likely he'll be ever to abandon me."

Even if the I-need-a-man-to-pay-my-way image does magnetize some men, actually having a man pay your way (or pad it, at any rate) can lead to disaster—for you more than for him.

I've heard tragic stories from many a woman who has given a man "the best years of my life" (in return for his financial support)—and he then departs, leaving her to fend for herself, middle-aged with no work experience. I've heard tales of widows who had no knowledge of money management being robbed blind by CPA's or "investment counselors" who were either inept or corrupt. In the absence of their husbands, on whom they always depended, these widows relied on other male authority figures—to their everlasting regret.

Today, we realize that any woman who does not learn how to look after herself financially—no matter what her age, or marital status—is sabotaging herself as surely as if she set a time bomb off under her bed. With the frequency of divorce nowadays, and the gap between the ages of death for men and women, every woman owes it to herself to learn to fend for herself financially. If she doesn't, she's exploitable—and only she, not society, not men, is responsible.

By way of illustrating the difference financial solvency and acuity makes in a woman's self-image, happiness, and lack of desperate dependence on men, let me tell you about two patients of mine. Both are in their forties. Both have never married.

Lisa is a former model who earned a fortune doing everything from magazine covers to television commercials. Unfortunately, Lisa did not manage her money wisely. She let an accountant handle her financial affairs, and he turned out to be inept. Lisa's modeling jobs are not as frequent nor as lucrative as they were when she was younger. She's been trying to find another career, but so far she has not been successful.

Lisa is always broke, and she is quite unhappy. "If only I had gotten married," Lisa sighs, "I'd have someone to take care of me." She is in active pursuit of a husband, convinced that a husband is the answer. And, of course, husband material of the caliber Lisa requires is hard to come by, she finds. "All the good men are taken," she told me.

Phyllis, a television producer, has an entirely different attitude. She has invested her money in ways that paid off; one investment is the elegant townhouse she lives in. She can afford to entertain her friends lavishly, to buy gifts for her family and friends, to treat herself well by taking wonderful trips, buying exactly the clothes she wants, going to plays and concerts, buying a new car instead of sinking money into an old wreck like Lisa does.

Phyllis does not discount the possibility of getting married, should she meet someone she wants to marry. But she is in no rush. She's not out headhunting. "I don't need a man to support me," she says, "and that's a wonderful situation. Because when I do find someone I love, I'll get married—if I get married—out of want, not need."

Making lots of money is not, in itself, a guarantee of undependence. Knowing how to manage the money you make is equally, if not more, important.

I have a friend, Karen, whose mother forced her to go to business school when she was nineteen years old. Her mother said, "Even if you don't use it to make money right now or in the future—even if you get married and never work—every woman should know as much as there is to know about money."

Karen did go to business school. She got married when she was twenty-three, and she was a whiz at balancing her checkbook. But there wasn't much to balance since she was a free-lance artist and her husband was a free-lance photographer. Karen tired of the artist-in-a-garret life-style faster than her husband did. She convinced him that they should start a business, something solid, something more reliable than free-lance creativity.

So they opened a hot dog stand with every cent they had. Soon they were able to start another hot dog stand. Then they opened two more stands and hired some people to run them. Today, they have a chain of fast-food restaurants, franchises—and their considerable income was made possible, in part, by Karen's business acumen.

And the security of knowing that she can always take care of herself has helped Karen psychologically, too. Although she has a good marriage and says it wouldn't be fair to conjecture whether or not she'd be okay without her husband, my guess is that Karen would survive beautifully on her own.

It's clear that despite the depressing statistics of women's salaries versus men, many women have managed to make excellent incomes and/or make the most of whatever they earn. Anyone who truly wants to be financially independent can do it.

One of my favorite success stories is that of Helen Gurley Brown, who turned the then-languishing-*Cosmopolitan* magazine into one of the biggest-selling publications in the country. But before revamping *Cosmo*, she wrote *Sex and the Single Girl*, in which she recalled taking her lunch to the office in a brown paper bag when she was a secretary in Los Angeles and saving enough money so that she could buy her own Mercedes-Benz.

This is a classic story of—"It would be wonderful to have a husband, but since I don't right now, I'm going to make sure that I have the wonderful car of my dreams and the clothes I want—everything I want. I can get all those things myself."

And this was way before women's liberation.

Now we come to the trickiest part of being truly supportive of yourself. Financial security does give you a great measure of inner security. But just because you're earning money and managing it wisely does not mean that you're getting everything from your work that you possibly could.

Your work, ideally, can give you, in addition to an income, a creative outlet. It can be a source of pride. It may make you feel worthwhile. It can preoccupy you enough so that you are neither bored nor burdened by empty time in which to ruminate on the man in your life or to wish there were a man in your life.

But for all too many of my patients, work is simply a way to make a living. This is as true for men, incidentally, as it is for women.

Part of the problem is the emphasis, today, on *not* working. Our society, once devoted to the Puritan work ethic, is now governed more by the leisure time principle. People live for their vacations. They look forward to retirement, to the time when they can do nothing but putter around a golf course, loll on tropical beaches, read Proust from start to finish.

And the reason that leisure—a vacation or retirement or even getting a cold and being able to stay home and watch the "soaps" for a few days—is so appealing is that work, in many cases, is so unappealing. Very few people are fortunate enough to earn their living doing something they love.

The song "Nine to Five" was popular because it was the story of most peoples' lives—particularly women's.

You get up in the morning and have a hit of coffee and go to the office and everyone's putting you down and the whole world's on your case, especially your boss—and that's it.

Millions of people bought that record because they identified with that negative job image, the *Sturm and Drang* you go through in order to pay your rent in order to live.

This situation is particularly critical for women because, in addition to falling prey, like men, to the notion that idleness is idyllic, we are susceptible to an additional notion that keeps us from making the most of the work we do: Women are *supposed to* be more romantic than men—so romantic that, when it comes to work, we have a much harder time concentrating than men do.

One of my patients put it this way: "Men are obsessed with their work; women are obsessed with men."

Many a patient has asked me how men can be so work-oriented, given the general "unpleasantness" of work. "What is their secret?" ask my patients (willing, they maintain, but unable to fall in love with their jobs or careers).

There is really no big mystery about how to become involved in your work, involved to the point where work is a valuable resource for self-fulfillment and a means of relying less on men for attention, entertainment, money, and even power.

The secret is: You get out of your work what you put into it. My typical patient, upon hearing this, will say, "Oh, really? Well, why don't you trade places with me for a day. Why don't you be Mr. Tyrant's secretary. I'd like to see how much you'd be able to put into all that shuffling of papers, typing, taking dictation . . ."

My response to this patient, who thinks she is optionless, is that she has plenty of alternatives:

1. She can, in her spare time between paper-shuffling duties, learn as much about Mr. Tyrant's business as she can. She can think about the memos she's taking, the deal letters she's typing.

Then, when it seems to her that Mr. Tyrant is making a mistake, or when she thinks that another course of action would prove more profitable to the boss than the one he's taking, she can express her opinions to Mr. Tyrant. And, possibly, Mr. Tyrant will conclude that he needs a new secretary, that his present secretary's talents could be better put to use in the marketing department.

2. If Mr. Tyrant's line of work is boring to her, or if, after she offers several suggestions, he ignores her—she can spend her lunch hours looking for a job with more growth potential.

3. She can decide, "Okay, I'm not happy here with Mr. Tyrant. I know I've got great talent as a writer (or inventor or singer or photographer), but I need the money. So I'll grit my teeth and stick it out here while developing my *true* career at night and on weekends."

If you are not getting satisfaction from your job and if the job is certifiably dead-end, then the thing to do is to find out what you *do* love, and do everything in your power to turn that into your livelihood.

Sarah, one of my patients, is an accomplished guitar player and singer. But the gigs with bands are few and far between. So Sarah works as a cocktail waitress in a nightclub—in an establishment where many music executives and major musicians hang out so that, perhaps, she'll make a contact while earning her bread and butter.

Sarah could well let herself resent waitressing— after all, she's gifted; she feels that waiting on tables is demeaning. But she actually finds that she looks forward to going to work. She's involved in finding out who all the customers are—one of them might give her her big break. And she enjoys studying even the nonmusic business customers, hearing bits of their conversations, because Sarah's chronic people-watching is her source of inspiration for many songs she composes.

Quite a few of my patients are writers—and writing is a profession whose practitioners frequently earn a living doing something else, everything from cab driving to teaching to keypunch operating. And their minds, as they go about their unchallenging jobs, are usually busy planning the next paragraph or chapter of the opus sitting in their typewriters. The jobs are bearable because they finance the writing.

"But I'm not a writer or musician," many of my patients say. "I've got no special talent. And my job is a bore. I'm really stuck."

In this case, if you feel "stuck" in a dull job, you have two alternatives. One is to try and scrap the "stuck" attitude and force yourself to see the job in a more positive light. The other, as I suggested, is to find more fulfilling work, not necessarily in the form of another job but perhaps in capitalizing on some talent you may not even know you have.

Let's look at what reasons you might have for adopting a more positive attitude toward a boring job. First of all, if the job is fairly lucrative and offers a chance for advancement, you can adopt the attitude: "All this drudgery is worth it because it is enabling me to dress well, take cabs instead of the bus, eat steak five times a week, reupholster my thrift shop chaise longue in raw silk, etc."

My friend Karen is an example of how keeping your gradually improving life-style firmly in mind can help you endure even the dullest daily routine. When she and her husband began their hot dog stand that led to the fast-food chain, they worked sixteen hours a day, seven days a week. The work was not scintillating, either—finding suppliers, figuring prices according to food and labor costs, standing in the hot sun peddling their wares, tending to never-ending lists of boring details. "It was not exactly creatively satisfying," Karen says, "for either of us."

Today, with the business having grown to a restaurant chain, Karen still does not find the day-to-day work fascinating. "But I grit my teeth and carry on," she says, "because all the grueling little chores I do every day keep the quality of our operation high. And the better we serve the public, the more we earn and the better we live.

"Also," Karen continues, "I get satisfaction out of serving *good* food to people. It's more trouble—which means more grueling little chores—but satisfying customers makes me feel satisfied.

"And there is a measure of gratification, too, in knowing that you did every one of those grueling little chores to the best of your ability."

This is true of any job—even when you are not your own boss and buoyed by the prospect of being a self-made millionaire. Take a job that would seem, to the observer, unendurably dull—being a worker on an automobile assembly line, fitting the same part on the same engine day after day. Yet I have known assembly line workers in various types of factories who get great satisfaction from doing their work flawlessly. They are proud, too, of the final product to which they contributed.

And I have known office workers who, instead of complaining inwardly about the dreariness of their typing, steno, filing or bookkeeping duties, take pride in the fact that by carrying out their tasks efficiently, they contribute to a smoothly running office and make other people's work easier.

They enjoy being part of the team, helping the team to accomplish its objectives.

Marian, the secretary of a midwestern politician, describes her job as "the constant scheduling and rescheduling of his appointments, letter writing, memo making, stamp licking, Xeroxing, phone calling. Item by item, it's hardly glamorous. There's nothing glamorous about politics on the grass roots, day-today level. I don't even think it's too glamorous to my boss.

"But I just keep thinking 'I'm an important cog in this particular political wheel.' I think 'my labors here at the Xerox machine could mean the difference between winning and losing the election.' I don't literally think that all the time, but that's the general attitude that I bring to work.

"And I feel really good about my job—and about myself."

Now we come to the second alternative for women who feel trapped in a dull job: If there is no way to approach the job in a more positive way, try to approach the whole concept of working more creatively in order to find work that is fulfilling.

The main reason that my women patients often remain in jobs they regard as dead-end is that they feel they are "not talented enough" or "not creative enough" to do better. Or, often enough, they have no idea of what work they might enjoy more.

But everyone has some untapped creative ability.

And, frequently, discovering a craft or other pursuit that you love doing—independent of work—can lead to it becoming your work.

Francine is a woman who thought she had no talent. Not only did she consider herself a creative zero, she put herself down for having "failed" at marriage, too. She was collecting child support and alimony from her ex-husband. But this made her feel like a welfare case. She not only couldn't stand accepting money from this man who had been a philanderer throughout their marriage but she wanted to have a career; she wanted to be "someone" on her own.

A couple that Francine knew was having a party for their daughter in honor of her college graduation. They asked Francine, who was an excellent cook, to cater the party. Francine did so well that several guests at the party asked her to cater their parties—and Francine was on her way to a thriving catering business.

She then applied for, and received, a small business loan and rented one floor of an office building with a kitchen that she remodeled. She now has a growing list of clients, a growing staff, and—best of all—work she truly loves. She had always invented her own recipes—but she never thought this was worth more than compliments from her family. Now she has capitalized on a talent she never even regarded as such— and she's turned her life around.

Many women overlook the talent they may be demonstrating in their hobbies. They consider knitting, for example, "a pastime" or "an economy measure"— because knitwear is cheaper to make than to buy.

But your needlepoint or knitting or crocheting or sewing skills can lead to a fairly substantial business— and this work is something that can be done from your own home. I know of several women who run virtual custom design studios in their living rooms, creating one-of-a-kind dresses, satchels, sweaters, sweatercoats—you name it.

One woman whose passion was needlepoint progressed from making Christmas pillow-covers for friends to running a thriving business selling the patterns she designs, stencils, and packages with yarn and tools—her own custom-made do-it-yourself kits (encouraging the creativity of other women).

My three favorite sweaters were knitted for me by a woman who has a loom in her home and makes quite a good income custom designing and selling knits to an increasing number of customers. She doesn't advertise; her business has boomed through word of mouth. She has no overhead. Her clients feel as if they are getting bargains—and they are, because sweaters in the stores not only cost more but they're not as well made. This woman earns enough from the clothes she designs and makes so that she does not need a bread-and-butter job.

The number of women who support themselves entirely or partially with their own cottage industries has grown enormously in recent years. The vast variety of arts and crafts that women market is evident in cooperative shops such as The Hired Hand in Manhattan, which sells crafts on consignment. Merchandise includes quilts, quilted clothes, potholders, tie-dyed and hand-painted T-shirts, jewelry, baskets, hand-carved wooden objects, etc.

Craftspeople do not make enormous amounts of money, as a rule. But the mere fact that you are more profitably involved in your real work (potting or painting or whatever) can make the job you do to pay the rent, the one you consider a bore, more bearable. What helps even more is identifying yourself according to this "real work." For instance, a woman I know who spends every evening and every weekend in the pottery, but who actually earns a living bookkeeping, says, "I am a potter" when people ask what she does.

Two of the most spectacularly successful women I can think of started businesses not from their hobbies or artistic talents but from their efforts to improve themselves. Jean Nidetch developed an eating plan that enabled her to lose weight and keep it off. And then she parlayed this plan into Weight Watchers, Inc., which now consists not only of therapy groups throughout the country but also restaurants, a packaged-foods division, and a magazine. Jacquelyn Rogers couldn't stop smoking—until she worked out a behavior modification technique for herself that worked. She then founded Smokenders in order to pass this technique on to other people who couldn't stop smoking.

These women not only helped themselves—they're helping millions of other people. Imagine how satisfying that must be!

Work has become the most important part of life for an increasing number of women—whether or not they are involved with men or hope to be involved with men. It is crucial that every woman start to take work more seriously—because, when you come right down to it, work is the only thing that is entirely yours. It belongs to you. It reflects you. And this is something that you can never—or should never—say about the man you love.

Conclusion

You're now on your way to undependence!

You've seen that you do not desperately need a man for sex, security (emotional or financial), companionship—or for any reason at all.

If you are not involved with a man right now, you know that there is no reason to postpone creating a life-style and living life to the hilt until you find Mr. Right.

If you have found Mr. Right, you know that it is not his presence that makes you the wonderful person you are. You know that your happiness, fulfillment, and feelings of self-worth pivot around your own inner core of security. Your life need not revolve around him.

If your relationship with Mr. Right should come to an end for some reason—or if you are on your own and think you'll stay that way—you now know, for sure, that this does not mean that you are doomed to be lonely, depressed, dissatisfied, or to be pitied by the world at large.

You know all these things. Now it is up to you to put this knowledge into action, to dump those old attitudes that kept you trapped in the desperately dependent mold, to act on your new attitude: "It may be great to be half a couple, but the best thing is knowing

180 °

that I am a whole person no matter what my marital status."

You might identify, now, with something a patient said to me recently. Cynthia was leaving therapy because she and I both felt that she had accomplished her goals of knowing herself better, liking herself better—and not clinging to her husband for either a sense of who she was or the feeling that she was loved. Cynthia's extreme reliance on her husband had been destroying the relationship.

As she left my office for the last time, Cynthia said to me, "Dr. Russianoff, I feel like I'm on much steadier ground now. And because of that, my marriage is on much steadier ground. I know it sounds like a contradiction in terms to say that the key to keeping a relationship wonderful is knowing that you *could* live without it—and happily—but I now know that that's true.

"But I'm a little bit nervous about the new me. Last night for instance, I was studying." (One of the consequences of Cynthia's new self-knowledge is that she quit her unsatisfying job in public relations and went to law school, something she always wanted to do and never felt capable of before.)

"I was studying for the exam—some cases in which I was particularly interested, in fact. But suddenly, I just broke off in midsentence and wandered over to Bob, who was reading the newspaper, and whispered 'Do you love me?'—just like the old me always did.

"But I guess if I only have a relapse like that every so often, instead of the syndrome dominating my life, I'm still batting a thousand. Right?"

I assured Cynthia that she was, indeed, right. Deeply engrained habits—particularly a habit such as thinking you are nothing without a man, which determines your whole self-image—do not disappear the minute you become aware that you can change and become cognizant of the ways in which you can change.

The important thing is that you are trying to change. Congratulate yourself on your progress; don't put yourself down every time you slip from your appointed course.

I told Cynthia what I wish I could say, personally, to every one of my readers: "You're on your own now. And I know you can handle it. And I know you share my confidence in you.

"Remember that if you need a pep talk, I'm right here. But also remember that the person who can help you the most, the person who knows you best and loves you the most, is you! If you truly believe this and act on it and avail yourself of *you*—your most valuable resource—then there is nothing else that I can tell you. You've got it made!"

Bibliography

The following material is geared to helping women develop more self-awareness. This is a brief list—many more books could be added—but the ones that have most strongly influened my writing of this book are included.

Political, Cultural and Sociological Influences

de Beauvior, Simone: *The Second Sex*, Alfred A. Knopf, Inc., 1952

Friedan, Betty: *The Feminine Mystique*, W. W. Norton & Co., Inc., 1963

Friedan, Betty: *It Changed My Life*, Random House, Inc., 1976

Friedan, Betty: *The Second Stage*, Summit Books, 1981

Greer, Germaine: *The Female Eunuch*, McGraw-Hill Books, 1971

Millett, Kate: *Flying*, Alfred A. Knopf, Inc., 1974

Millett, Kate: *Sexual Politics*, Avon Books, 1971

Williams, Juanita H.: *Psychology of Women*, W. W. Norton and Co., 1977

Female Psycho-Social Issues

Chesler, Phyllis: *Women and Madness*, Avon Books, 1973

Clanton, Gordon, and Smith, Lynn G., editors: *Jealousy*, Prentice-Hall, Inc., 1977

Dowling, Collette: *The Cinderella Complex*, Summit Books, 1981

Friday, Nancy: *My Mother, My Self*, Dell Publishing Co., 1977

Friedman, Martha: *Overcoming The Fear of Success*, Seaview Books, 1980

Halas, Celia, and Matteson, Roberta: *I've Done So Well— Why Do I Feel So Bad?* Macmillan Publishing Co., 1978; this book illustrates the paradoxes which confuse and bind women in all relationships.

Horney, Karen: *Neurosis and Human Growth*, W. W. Norton and Co., 1950

James, Muriel, and Jongeward, Dorothy: *Born to Win*, Addison-Wesley Publishers, 1971; see particularly chapter 4 on "scripting" and the accompanying exercises.

Kundsin, Ruth B.: *Women and Success*, William Morrow and Co., 1974

Miller, Jean Baker: *Toward A New Psychology of Women*, Beacon Press, 1976

Missildine, W. Hugh: *Your Inner Child of the Past*, Simon & Schuster, Inc., 1963

Pogrebin, Letty Cottin: *Growing Up Free*, McGraw-Hill, 1980

Smith, Manuel J.: *Kicking the Fear Habit*, Dial Press, 1978

Female Biological Issues

Boston Women's Health Book Collective, ed.: *Our Bodies, Ourselves*, revised edition, Simon & Schuster, Inc., 1979

Manipulation By Men

Harragan, Betty Lehan: *Games Mother Never Taught You*, Rawson Associates Publishers, 1977

Hennig, Margaret, and Jardim, Anne: *The Managerial Woman*, Simon & Schuster, Inc., 1976

Shostrum, Everett L: *Man the Manipulator*, Abingdon Press, 1967

Walker, Leonore E.: *The Battered Woman*, Harper and Row, 1979

Women in Sex and Love

Barbach, Lonnie G.: *For Yourself: The Fulfillment of Female Sexuality*, Doubleday and Co., 1975

Comfort, Alex: *The Facts of Love*, Crown, 1979

Comfort, Alex: *The Joy of Sex*, Crown, 1972

Goldstine, Daniel, et al.: *The Dance-Away Lover*, William Morrow and Co., 1977

Hite, Shere: *The Hite Report: A Nationwide Survey on Female Sexuality*, Macmillan Publishing Co., 1976 (Note: Ms. Hite has recently published a work on male sexuality; you will need to be specific as to which volume you need when asking for it at your bookstore or library.)

Hodge, Marshall B.: *Your Fear of Love*, Doubleday and Co., 1967

Masters, William and Johnson, Virginia: *Human Sexual Response*, Little, Brown & Co., 1966

Women and Depression

Burns, David D.: *Feeling Good*, William Morrow and Co., 1980; be sure to do the suggested exercises.

Scarf, Maggie: *Unfinished Business*, Doubleday and Co., 1980

Seligman, Martin E. R.: *Helplessness*, W. H. Freeman and Co., 1975

Listening and Communication

Gottman, John, et al.: *A Couple's Guide to Communication*, Research Press, 1976

Satir, Virginia: *Conjoint Family Therapy*, Science and Behavior Books, 1967; particularly the two chapters on communication.

Moving Toward Change

Bloom. Lynn Z., Coburn, Karen, and Pearlman, Joan: *The New Assertive Woman*, Delacorte Press, 1975

Ellis, Albert and Harper, Robert A.: *A New Guide to Rational Living*, Prentice-Hall, Inc., 1975

Gallwey, W. Timothy: *The Inner Game of Tennis*, Random House Inc., 1974 (Note: Don't be misled by the use of the word "tennis" in the title; the book's ideas apply to dozens of areas.)

Jacobson, Edmund: *You Must Relax*, McGraw-Hill Books, 1934

Kennedy, Eugene: *If You Really Knew Me, Would You Still Like Me?*, Argus Communications, 1975

Powell, John: *Why Am I Afraid to Tell You Who I Am?*, Argus Communications, 1969

Welch, Mary Scott: *Networking*, Harcourt, Brace and Jovanovich, 1980

Williamson, Jane, editor, et al.: *Woman's Action Almanac*, William Morrow and Co., 1979

Career Development

Bolles, Richard: *What Color Is Your Parachute?*, Ten-Speed Press, 1972

Jackson, Tom: *The Perfect Resume*, Doubleday & Co., Inc., 1981

Recent Fiction Related to Female Experience

Alther, Lisa: *Kinflicks*, Alfred A. Knopf, Inc., 1976

French, Marilyn: *The Women's Room*, Summit Books, 1977

Kingston, Maxine Hong: *The Woman Warrior*, Random House, 1975

Morrison, Toni: *Tar Baby*, Alfred A. Knopf, Inc., 1980

Organizations

The National Organization of Women maintains chapters across the country. You can write to the national office at 425 Thirteenth Street NW, Suite 1048, Washington, D.C. 20004 to find the local chapter nearest you. NOW and its local chapters have information on consciousness-raising groups and how to start one. These groups, as well as being informative, can be supportive and a source of friendship. NOW and its local groups also sponsor interesting programs and workshops.

Women's Action Almanac, edited by Jane Williamson (listed above), has excellent listings of women's organizations in various fields and geographical locations. Here is a brief sample dealing with the battered woman, from p. 31:

National Communications Network for the Elimination of Violence Against Women
4520 44th Avenue South
Minneapolis, MN 55406

Resource Kit on Battered Women
Order from: Women's Bureau, Office of the Secretary
Department of Labor
Washington, D.C. 20210

"This packet includes an overview article, a run-down of the legislative issues, a program and resource dictionary. There are also guides to funding sources. An excellent collection."

The *Women's Action Almanac* itself costs $7.95 as of this printing, and if not available at your bookstore or library, it can be ordered by contacting the publisher:
Morrow Quill Paperbacks
105 Madison Avenue
New York, NY 10016

Networking, by Mary Scott Welch (also listed above) is full of examples of how women have been helpful to other women in the job market and in career changes. The book includes a directory of women's professional organizations.

The Help Book, by J. L. Barkas (published by Scribner's Sons, New York, 1979) contains hundreds of organizations and agencies of interest, listed by field or area of concern. It includes not only government agencies, but private organizations and foundations as well.

Network directories are also available in the March, 1980 issue of *Working Woman*, and by writing AGOG, Inc., P.O. Box 20121, Minneapolis, MN 55420.

ABOUT THE AUTHOR

DR. PENELOPE RUSSIANOFF is one of the nation's leading psychologists. She has been a faculty member at the New School for Social Research since 1960, teaching courses that range from "Assertiveness Training" to "Psychological Aspects of Weight Control" and "Risking Intimacy," a course she co-teaches with Dr. Herbert Freudenberger (author of Burn-Out). In 1978, Dr. Russianoff completed a ten-part TV series for NBC based on her New School course, "Risking Change." Dr. Russianoff is a member of several organizations including the American Psychological Association, and has won a number of awards for her educational and clinical work.